THE COMMUNITY COLLEGE LIBRARY
A PLAN FOR ACTION

THE COMMUNITY COLLEGE LIBRARY
A PLAN FOR ACTION

by
Helen Rippier Wheeler

The Shoe String Press, Inc.
Hamden, Connecticut
1965

Library of Congress Catalog Card Number: 65-16220

Printed in The United States of America

TABLE OF CONTENTS

LIST OF TABLES

ACKNOWLEDGMENTS

The investigation reported here is based in part on the author's project submitted in partial fulfillment of the requirements for the degree of Doctor of Education, Columbia University, Teachers College, 1964. Data for the study were collected from community college library directors who were generous with their time and assistance; particular gratitude is due Mrs. Alice Griffith, director of the Mohawk Valley Community College library. The Teachers College library staff, Mrs. Florence Wilkinson especially, have provided counsel and service. I would like to express my gratitude to Dr. Max Brunstetter, sponsor of the doctoral project, without whose valuable criticism and more valuable encouragement it would not have been completed.

And to Professor Maurice Tauber of the Columbia University School of Library Service — always wise, preceptive and stable in guiding and supporting both the project and the book — I offer my deepest gratitude.

INTRODUCTION

This is a report of an attempt to identify and describe the ways in which the community college library can and should best serve its unique institution's program.

The need for a guide to be used in connection with the development of library programs and with the implementation of the ALA junior college standards has been felt by community colleges especially because they endeavor to serve a variety of educational purposes by means of a combination of programs. Community college administrators, library directors and other faculty lack a systematically prepared description of the ways in which their libraries can support the unique functions and needs of their institutions, and of the means of providing these services. An analysis of such a description should have implications for the development of the elements of an appropriate library program when applied with flexibility.

The community college library faces a new period fraught with specialized problems. As part of a booming institution, it can go along with the tide only so far. The evolution and publication of the American Library Association's qualitative and quantitative junior college standards provide a foundation; next is the development of the unique community college library program. The following development of criteria for the community college library program, analysis of current practice, and making of specific recommendations may provide assistance.

Seven steps were taken in order to identify and describe the ways in which the community college library program can and should best serve its unique institution's program. They were: (1) investigation of the literature of the fields, (2) development of criteria for the general organization and

operation of the library of a community college, (3) development of a survey-questionnaire to secure information
regarding the ways in which library programs support
the unique needs and functions of ongoing community
college programs, (4) visits to several community colleges
to supplement the questionnaire, (5) analysis of current
community college library practice in terms of the previously established criteria especially, (6) recommendations
to the community college administrator and library director,
and (7) description of the "ideal" community college library
program which should be the ultimate goal.

Ten criteria for the general organization and operation
of the library program of a community college were evolved,
each supplemented by illustrative measures. They included
the areas of library collection and organization, program,
personnel, management, instruction and use, and evaluation. Validation of the criteria was based on reference to
proven practice and standard publications and tools in the
higher education, community college and professional
library service fields. The criteria were also submitted for
examination to leaders in the fields of library service and
the community college.

In order to obtain a picture of current community college
library practice, a questionnaire was developed and mailed
to the library directors of all public community colleges
founded before 1960 having enrollments of five hundred
or more students. The lack of a community college directory
or other standardized list made the structuring of the mail-
ing list difficult. In general, institutional selection was based
on age and enrollment as presented in the Junior College
Directory covering the period June 1960 — May 1961[1],
in combination with the major community college characteristics. The result was a list of one hundred ninety-eight
community colleges, in twenty-seven states, or 49% of all
public junior colleges. Early in 1963, each library director
received two copies of the questionnaire, a return stamped
envelope and a letter explaining the purpose of the study,
offering to send a summary of the results and assuring
personal and institutional anonymity. About a month later,
a reminder letter was mailed.

The criteria and their illustrative measures supplied the
guidelines for the construction of the questionnaire, a ten-

page instrument containing approximately one hundred fifty objective items (yes/no, multiple choice, statistics, etc.) and sixty-five subjective items (requesting comment, opinion, description, etc.) As with the criteria, all aspects of college library administration and community college library program relative to the study were touched upon. An effort was made to discourage any assumption that every question referred to desirable practice.

Three essay-type items were included in the development of the questionnaire. They were inquiries as to what the library director sees as the unique needs and functions of the community college movement and which characteristics apply to his own college program and its community, and the specific ways in which his library program assists in this undertaking; what, in his opinion, are the greatest problem areas in community college library programing in general, and in his institution; and what improvements he would like to incorporate into his library program of the future. Here he was asked to describe techniques, solutions to problems and innovations which he had found successful or observed in other community college libraries.

One hundred three completed questionnaires (55%) had been returned within three months. (Nine library directors replied that they did not consider that their institutions were functioning as community colleges at present, and one college had closed.) Some details of the response distribution are presented in **Tables 1 and 2.** Response tended to originate in urban institutions with enrollments of between five hundred and one thousand and founded between 1946 and 1950. It should be borne in mind, however, that although comprehensive in many ways, the questionnaire population limited itself to twenty-seven states. Also, the purpose of the questionnaire was not a minute statistical report, but, rather, a general picture of current community college library programing.

The following terminology has been employed:

Community College is designated as a movement rather than an institution. The terms community, junior, general college, technical institution, extension center, undergraduate center are really all of a piece in the general movement

to extend to large numbers of people the advantages of
education and the kinds of education they need and want.
The President's Commission on Higher Education desig-
nates the general movement as "Community colleges . . .
community centered . . . community serving."

TABLE 1

DISTRIBUTION OF QUESTIONNAIRES TO 198
COMMUNITY COLLEGE LIBRARIES AND THE
RESPONSE BY REGIONS AND STATES OF THE
UNITED STATES OF AMERICA

Region & State	# of Colleges Receiving	# of Colleges Responding	# Reported Not Applicable
Middle States	**21**	**14**	1
Maryland	4	4	
New Jersey	1	1	
New York	16	9	1
New England	**2**	**1**	
Massachusetts	2	1	
Western	**56**	**32**	
California	56	32	
Southern	**51**	**23**	5
Florida	11	8	
Georgia	6	3	2
Kentucky	1	1	
Mississippi	6	-	
North Carolina	2	-	1
Texas	25	11	2
North Central	**55**	**27**	4
Arizona	2	2	
Colorado	4	2	
Illinois	14	7	1
Iowa	2	2	
Kansas	5	2	
Michigan	14	5	1 closed
Minnesota	4	2	

Region & State	# of Colleges Receiving	# of Colleges Responding	# Reported Not Applicable
Missouri	3	1	
North Dakota	1	1	
Oklahoma	4	1	2
Wisconsin	1	1	
Wyoming	1	1	
Northwest	**13**	**6**	
Alaska	1	1	
Idaho	1	1	
Utah	1	-	
Washington	10	4	
Total	**198**	**103**	**10**

TABLE 2

ENROLLMENT OF RESPONDING
COMMUNITY COLLEGES

Enrollment	# of community colleges	% of community colleges
under 1,000	45	43.6%
1,001-2,000	23	22.3
2,001-3,000	8	7.7
3,001-4,000	9	8.7
4,001-5,000	8	7.7
5,001-6,000	3	2.9
6,001-7,000	1	.9
7,001-8,000	2	1.9
8,001-9,000	1	.9
9,001-10,000	2	1.9
over 10,000	1	.9
	Total 103	100%

The institutions considered to be functioning as community colleges for the purposes of this study were almost
all public junior colleges, co-educational, with low or no

tuition, without religious affiliation, offering terminal technical programs as well as courses which could be equated with the lower division of senior college work. In addition, there would be some general education and "adult education" courses available for persons not involved in any particular program, and a strong emphasis on guidance and counseling. A community served could be defined and there was an established relationship with that community in planning and services. Generally, admission was based on proven need, maturity, or simple graduation from high school. The majority of students were day students.

Library materials are printed and non-printed materials, including audio visual, relating in any way to the goals of the over-all college program; especially instructional materials and books.

Librarian refers to a professional librarian who has completed a professional library service training program. He satisfies state and local certification requirements which are applicable to his community college.

Library director is a professional librarian, with the Master's degree from an accredited library school, following a BA degree in liberal arts. His professional training, experience and personality should qualify him for administrative, instructional and leadership responsibilities; the person in charge of the community college library program, and in most cases, the questionnaire respondent.

Administrator refers to the person in charge of the community college, whose authority usually is derived from the governing board and to whom the library director may be responsible. This use of the term is consistent with the great variety of titles provided by the questionnaire population, e.g. president, dean, superintendent, principal or director.

Library orientation refers to an introductory library experience sometimes provided for new students at the beginning of each term. It typically consists of a tour of the library or, possibly, a library unit in a freshman English course. (See also **Library instruction** and **Library technology.**)

Library instruction may consist of visits to a class by a librarian, upon teacher-request, for instruction in the use of the library's resources in the aspect of the subject currently being studied. It may also consist of the more formal, scheduled course, meeting typically once a week for one elective credit. It should be distinguished from **Library orientation.** (See also **Library orientation** and **Library technology.**)

Library technology refers to the recent community college development in the vocational training of clerical library personnel. It is, therefore, a terminal curriculum in itself and may consist of a sequence of technical courses integrated with the college requirements in general education and lead to one of the junior college associate degrees. It is not a program for the training of librarians. (See also **Library orientation** and **Library instruction.**)

Chapter I

BACKGROUND AND FUNCTIONS OF THE COMMUNITY COLLEGE

The American community is a changing one — changes in population structure, technology, occupational patterns and mores have combined with national and international developments to make community life at all levels more complex. The advance of technology has the effect of upgrading some workers to higher levels of training and skills with increased pay, as well as bringing more women onto the employment scene; at the same time, automation may throw others out of jobs. There are increased educational requirements resulting from the improved standard of living and competition. A large proportion of the population has time and money for a higher living standard, but lacking the ability to enjoy and profit from it, the individual may become a social liability. The demands upon education are continually increasing in terms of both preparation for employment and the personal requirements for living in a world where international understanding is essential to life itself.

There is need for a revised educational concept which can serve both young and older adults by providing for many of their post-high school needs. The community-centered junior college has become the solution in many areas of the United States. Its function may be fulfilled in such services and activities as conferences and consultation, as well as in the classroom and library. It offers a multi-purpose, comprehensive program of higher education. Contained typically in a community, junior, public college are courses in liberal arts, mainly for transfer to a senior college, with the Associate in Arts degree incentive; semi-professional and technical terminal programs often with the Associate in Science or Applied Science degree; and adult-education-type courses and programs.

Historically, the junior college has functioned as the first two years of the university or as a continuation of high school. With the passage of time, new needs have become apparent, and the junior college has acquired responsibility for occupational training beyond high school, and, recently, for the continuing education of the American people. It is now referred to as a community college because it serves the post-high school needs of the local community in which it is situated. However, there are still public and private junior colleges which concentrate on preparing the student for transfer to a senior college, and which have not assumed the broader functions of vocational training, guidance and adult education that characterize the community college.

The history of the movement of American education into the community college field is well demonstrated in such states as California, New York and Florida. In California, junior colleges have experienced great growth. As early as 1907, permissive legislation made possible the first public junior college (at Fresno, in 1910); today, the community junior college is an integral part of California public education. Elsewhere, technical institutes, extension centers, and adult education programs have evolved into community colleges. Recent years have also seen the establishment of completely new institutions, such as Orange County Community College in Middletown, New York. The Higher Education Facilities Act of 1963 authorized expenditure over the next five years of $1.2 billion for facilities construction by colleges and universities. Public junior colleges are eligible for approximately $50 million annually for general construction in federal grants authorized for the first three years of the program, with funds to be allocated on a matching basis to the various states.

In modern American society, it has become apparent that high school education is often not enough. More and more people need and want more and more education in order to compete and advance on the job, to function as an informed citizenry and to provide a better home life.

It is the unique function of the community college to make post-high school education available to people of all ages and experiential background by providing instruction locally at little or no cost. Related to this is the fact that more members of the college-age group are now entering college. It is one of the community college's unique functions to relieve post-high school enrollment pressure, while at the same time democratizing higher education by means of its lowered costs, accessibility and curricular innovations. Many more college students can be served than would have otherwise been possible if students in the community faced an alternative of traveling some distance to a college where expenses were considerable and where typically a full program of liberal arts subjects is carried by young people in a specific age range.

Students have different kinds of abilities, and many fail in traditional kinds of academic work. They may be able students, but they are not all able in the abstract, academic sense in which selected students of the past generation excelled in college. The community college attempts to provide the kinds of curricula and guidance which will answer the problems of people who leave school with only part of an education and a sense of failure. These include technical programs which can develop skills and make possible gainful and interesting careers. In addition, the community college provides the opportunity for dropouts to rediscover and reestablish themselves, to feel free to explore what is available to them in the community college environment.

Because it offers a variety of programs and welcomes a variety of interests and abilities, one of the unique functions of the community college has become the provision of a strong guidance program. The community college helps the student to understand himself and to take advantage of available opportunities for education, job advancement and self-realization.

Over the years, the community junior college has taken on new functions, but traditionally it also offers lower-division college training. There is a great deal of evidence that junior college transfers can do well in senior colleges. [3,4,5] Therefore, it is another unique function of the community college to provide a low cost, accessible, lower-division college experience of transfer caliber. In effect, this function also democratizes higher education by making it possible for many more people to attend college.

The community college typically surveys its community to identify those types of semi-professional work which demand education of less than four years duration beyond high school. In cooperation with educators, businessmen, industrialists, and other members of the community, it functions to develop and provide courses, curricula and services combining occupational training and general education which are genuine collegiate programs needed in the community.

With less emphasis placed on the responsibility for fundamental research and publication, the community college faculty can concentrate on high quality teaching. Often the student body has a mixture of abilities and experiential backgrounds. Aided and encouraged by competent, enthusiastic and well-selected teachers who understand and support the unique functions of the community college, students are more likely to become self-propelled and to carry themselves on toward graduation, graduate work and satisfying employment than had they not had the opportunity for work in a typically smaller institution.

Community colleges, then, usually have in common five characteristics growing out of their unique functions. They cost the student relatively little to attend. Most high school graduates and adults can be admitted. The objectives and curricula are comprehensive and include lower-division-type and general education courses as well as programs of an occupational nature for those who do not plan to transfer to a senior college. Students with subject and academic deficiencies are assisted through special remedial classes and work, and considerable emphasis is placed on guidance and counseling of students who have not made firm decisions regarding their educational and vocational plans.

The Background of the Library in the Community College Program

The community college instructional program is unique in its broad functions and in the needs of its students. Collections of library materials both printed and audio visual suited to these broad ranges of abilities, interests, experiences, instructional methods and curricula are needed by the com-

munity college student and teacher. There are also implications here for library personnel and services to administer
these materials and to develop their use.

Generally, the role of the community college library has
been conservative and traditional. It has usually provided
books for courses, to fill faculty requests, for a basic reference service and to a lesser extent, for the vocational, cultural and avocational enrichment of the students, to the
extent that staff, funds and support were available.

The library's function in relation to the total role of the
college's community service is an especially important one
to perform. Yet a recent survey of studies to determine
which areas in the two-year college field are receiving the
most and the least attention found that the area most neg-
lected was the library.[6] Three recently published books in
the field do not refer to the library.[7] A new edition of a
standard library tool devotes some attention to it, emphasizing the need for a large collection, the linking of library
practice more closely to the classroom (and vice versa),
and the problem of adequate staffing and quarters, and
concludes that:

> At present there are far too many junior college libraries
> housed in overcrowded and inadequate library quarters
> and too few full-time workers for the librarian to do a
> first-rate professional job.[8]

Over thirty years have passed since the Junior College
Round Table of the American Library Association suggested a set of minimum requirements for junior college
libraries. In 1930, emphasis was on quantitative consideration of such things as books, budget and staff. Some pro-
posals of that era, such as the recommended minimum of
two professional librarians, are still waiting for recognition.
Many other efforts to improve junior college libraries followed. By 1954, minimum tentative qualitative standards
in the form of recommendations had been prepared by the
Junior College Libraries Section of the Association of College and Research Libraries, a division of the American
Library Association.

The Association of College and Research Libraries has
published "ALA Standards for Junior College Libraries"[9],
designed to provide a guide for junior colleges, including

community college libraries. They cover functions, structure
and government, budget, staff, collections (including audio
visual materials), building, quality of service and its evaluation and inter-library cooperation. The concepts are those
of the library as the intellectual powerhouse of the junior
college and the junior college librarian as an educator. But,

> The (American Association of Junior Colleges') Com-
> mission on Administration does not approve of these
> statements as **standards** for junior college libraries, since
> these statements so labeled will undoubtedly be used for
> accreditation purposes.

> The Commission is in general agreement with the pur-
> pose and functions of junior college libraries as stated
> by the American Library Association. It finds itself
> in disagreement . . .

with the **Standards'** recommendations that the library director report to the president, the library budget consist of
at least 5% of the college budget, there be at least two
librarians, the library director have faculty status, the need
for a collection of at least 20,000 titles is crucial and the
library seating facilities provide for at least 25% of the total
enrollment. [10]

> At this writing (March 14, 1963) the Association has
> determined that it will engage someone in the junior
> college field to develop a set of guidelines for junior
> college libraries. [11]

No further effort to aid progress in junior college library
programing has been announced by the American Association of Junior Colleges. This fact and the specialized nature
of the community junior college and its library have pro-
duced THE COMMUNITY COLLEGE LIBRARY; A
PLAN FOR ACTION.

Chapter II

CRITERIA FOR THE
COMMUNITY COLLEGE LIBRARY PROGRAM

Almost all of the scant literature dealing with the community college library is in the form of periodical articles and theses and falls into the areas of standards and accreditation, materials and selection, state and local descriptions and reports, personnel qualifications, and relationships to instructional programs. Other sources of assistance in development of criteria for the successful community college library program include analysis of the unique functions and needs of the community college as an institution; ALA STANDARDS FOR JUNIOR COLLEGE LIBRARIES [12]; regional association accreditation standards several of which consider the community junior college; state departments of education, library and education group bulletins, e.g. the School Library Association of California recommends junior college library standards; opinion and work of professional community college personnel as expressed personally and in their writings and professional activities; and professional college library practice which has been validated in actual use. Analysis of the recurring elements of these source areas provides some basis for the development of criteria for the successful community college library program.

The progress of a profession is usually marked by the accumulation of an increasing number of generally accepted practices. As these practices are commonly approved, they are recognized as norms or standards and are regularly followed until more satisfactory methods are discovered. A measure of standardization thus characterizes normal development.[13]

Standards are frequently used in evaluating educational institutions and their programs and are often applied more to quantitative aspects than to qualitative results. At the other extreme is the vaguely stated generality which provides neither great assistance nor information for working purposes. Criteria for the community college library should, therefore, provide qualitative-but-functional considerations which can be utilized in evaluation as well as for goals.

The new junior college standards constitute a valuable basic tool for community college library directors and administrators because they are flexible, up-to-date, qualitative as well as quantitative in their approach and include community colleges in their scope. That "The Standards laid down in this document must always be interpreted in the light of the aims and needs of the institution of which the library is a part" is stressed.[14]

Nevertheless, criteria have been developed with the purpose of providing a list pertinent to the unique institution, the community junior college. The criteria and their measures have been constructed so that they are readily usable when applied to the community college library program. (The ALA Standards are not devoted exclusively to community colleges nor even public junior colleges. Although qualitative as well as quantitative in their approach, at times they tend toward quantitative considerations and, as standards, are minimal.) If a standard is an accepted or established rule, the term 'criterion' adds the implication of a test. It is intended that the criteria provide the means for judging the community college library program.

Community college library practice has been examined by means of a questionnaire based in part on the ALA Standards; the practice as determined from answers received has been judged by means of the criteria. Although ten separate criteria have been developed, their interrelationship should be kept in mind. Following validation of each criterion, illustrative measures of the extent to which it is a part of a library's program are suggested and described. The measures have been constructed as objectively as possible. If a substantial number receive a positive reply, or comments and descriptive statements indicate confirmation of the measure, there is a likelihood that the criterion is being met.

Both the criteria and their measures refer to aspects of library programing which are related to the unique functions of the community college. The existence of an advisory library committee, the elimination of obsolete and excessively-duplicated materials and an on-going inventory, for instance, are not specified measures, although these and others are sufficiently relevant to be included in the questionnaire employed to obtain a picture of current practice. Standards which apply to both community and other types of college libraries have been included when considered vital to progress. The criteria of the successful community college library program as discussed in this study are as follows:

1. The over-all library program reflects the curriculum, objectives and functions of the local community college.
2. There is provision for continuous evaluation of the community college library program by means of appropriate techniques and measures.
3. Within the limits of its resources and responsibilities, the community college library facilitates the research work and professional growth of the faculty.
4. Instructional experiences in library usage are provided as needed by the community college student body.
5. In addition to instructional experiences, the library sponsors other non-book, library-related activities in further efforts to reach the community college student.
6. The library serves the community college faculty and student body as the central collection of the college's resource materials.
7. The library collection and services are appropriate for any specialized functions of the local institution (e.g. technical programs.)
8. The library collection and services are appropriate for any non-curricular learning experiences of the local institution (e.g. vocational guidance.)
9. Arrangement and servicing of materials facilitate their use by community college students and faculty.
10. The library is administered efficiently and effectively within the policies of the local community college.

1. The over-all library program reflects the curriculum, objectives and functions of the local community college.

In many ways, the community college has developed on the basis of what has been found useful to new institutions in other areas of higher education. In the same way, the community college library program has developed out of what has become valid in the support of new collegiate library programs.

The community junior college has grown to include four basic functions: preparation for advanced study, vocational education, general education and community service; its unique, comprehensive function and student body also create need for a strong guidance program. The local community college derives its objectives from the needs of its particular community and carries them out in varying emphases on curricula and other techniques. Each has a responsibility for determining the degree of emphasis to be placed upon any one of these functions and appropriate means for its implementation. Likewise, the individual community college program must derive its objectives from the institution of which it is a part and administer them with regard for proven college library practice.

Construction of the library program is dependent upon knowledge of the characteristics of the community college served, in the same manner that the college itself studies its community. The nature of the institution makes this an on-going task. The individual community college library has the basic duty of curricula-related book supply combined with as many other services and functions as have been identified. For example, transfer students should be provided with materials in the areas of their prospective majors. Technology programs may profit from the support of special audio visual materials. Vocational and guidance materials collections — well organized and serviced — may be utilized by community college guidance personnel and their clientele. Emphasis on library orientation and instruction eases the national situation, one in which the community college student is typically deficient. (Substandard library provision exists in many types of institutions today — school and public library services notably. [15]) Study of community needs may identify lack of technical and clerical library personnel which may be alleviated by a library technology curriculum.

Two decades ago, in one of the early works on the junior college library, Adams concluded that:

> Evaluation cannot precede program, but program must be preceded by plan; and the plan must recognize two essentials: first, that any library program must be organized in terms of the needs of a particular institution; second, that the program must be flexible and adaptable to new needs as they develop.[16]

Some illustrative measures of the first criterion are:
(1) The community college library is the result of planning begun at least one year before first classes.
(2) It is cooperatively planned by community college faculty, administration, students and interested laymen.
(3) It reflects an on-going approach, as evidenced by the existence of procedural innovations.
(4) There is a written report of a survey on which the library program of the new community college was based.

2. There is provision for continuous evaluation of the community college library program by means of appropriate techniques and measures.

The dynamic nature of the community college and its close community tie make continuous evaluation of the individual curricula, objectives and functions necessary. As they are revised, the library program should reflect the changes.

Quantitative measures and statistics have significance when applied flexibly, realistically and in balance with qualitative considerations. They continue to be effective in helping library and college administrators see their libraries realistically, by indicating areas where improvement is needed. They have been especially useful in areas of library personnel, collection, finances, quarters and equipment.

A continuous evaluation of the library's contribution to the community college program can be a cooperative endeavor of the professional library staff and other faculty.

An advisory library committee can, under certain circum-
stances, be a force for continuous evaluation of library
resources and services. Often, older community colleges and
their libraries would benefit from professional surveys and
publication of the results.

Some illustrative measures of the second criterion are:
(1) A library consultant is employed in preplanning.
(2) The current library program has been evaluated
    by a library consultant whose report consists of a
    professional library survey, the results of which are
    being published and implemented.
(3) Guidelines for evaluation provided by the "ALA
    Standards for Junior College Libraries" are utilized.
(4) Specific recommendations of accrediting or super-
    visory agencies have been published and are being
    carried out.

**3. Within the limits of its resources and responsibilities,
the community college library facilitates the research work
and professional growth of the faculty.**

A two-year program may lack emphases on such things
as research, graduate study, strong liberal arts departments
with majors' interests and professorial faculty. Often it is
necessary to recruit part-time teachers and others from
outside the field to provide for such things as specialized
technology programs, evening courses and unpredictable
enrollments. If these people are to be encouraged to become better teachers, the community college library will
recognize the need for well-selected and ample collections
of current and basic materials, including journals, in their
subject matter fields as well as in education.

The ALA Standards recommend that the library, beyond
its basic responsibilities:

. . . bring strong intellectual stimulation to both faculty
and students. It should help the faculty to keep abreast
of the progress of scholarship . . . The collection . . .
should be selected and organized so as to promote
and strengthen the teaching program in all of its aspects.
It should also seek to aid faculty members in their professional and scholarly growth. [17]

It has been shown that most college teachers lack time

and many lack bibliographical expertise to make the most
of the library's potential contribution to teaching, and there
is ample evidence that the traditional college instructor fails
to exploit fully the library's resources.[18] Extensive and
varied materials geared to faculty interest place in their
environment a possible means for improvement of·this
situation.

Some illustrative measures of the third criterion are:

(1) The community college library has teachers' ma-
     terials in their subject areas as well as in such fields
     as education, audio visual, community college, guid-
     ance, community study methodology, administration
     and curriculum.
(2) It subscribes to and has back files of THE JUNIOR
     COLLEGE JOURNAL, outstanding professional
     journals in all academic areas including education,
     and popular periodicals.
(3) It is involved in inter-library cooperation in behalf
     of community college faculty and staff.
(4) It distributes news bulletins, book lists and notifica-
     tion of acquisition of books of individual interest or
     recommendation.
(5) It expedites recommendations made by faculty for
     library materials acquisition.

**4. Instructional experiences in library usage are provided
as needed by the community college student body.**

Recent investigations demonstrate that basic library attitudes and skills stem directly from the classroom, i.e. the
instructor's attitude and skill in integrating library use
with coursework are the mose important means of fostering library usage. One investigation further suggests that
the student uses the library in a way which reflects his
instructors' concepts of what the library has to offer: limited
student use of the library may follow limited understanding
of its potential contributions to coursework. It indicates
that conventional instruction in college library use is largely ineffective.[19]

In the case of the community college library, these facts
emphasize the librarian's need to persevere in the use of
the techniques at his disposal. While endeavoring to influence
faculty, faculty-hiring administrators and teachers colleges

to recognize the implications for their activities, he must exploit library orientation and other instructional experiences to provide for some of the students' needs and rights.

It is incumbent upon the community college library to provide both expanded library orientation **and** library instruction. The need for provision in its program of the combination of the two distinct functions is intensified by the varied backgrounds and abilities of community college students. Often the community college is fed by high schools which provide little or no library backgrounds. Older adults frequently had no library experience in high school or they may have forgotten it, especially if the public library is inactive or distant.

Considerable space is devoted in the syllabus, THE LIBRARY IN COLLEGE INSTRUCTION [20] to consideration of ways that librarians and teachers can help the college function as a teaching instrument. The Southern Association of Colleges and Secondary Schools, as another example, has been active in pointing out the need for cooperation among librarians, faculty and administration, but it also stresses that, while librarians have the obligation of selecting the most useful materials and of keeping service responsive to curricular needs, the teaching faculty are ultimately responsible for the intelligent use of library materials. The degree to which the college lives up to its proper function depends not only upon needed books and good service, but also upon the demands which are made upon it by the faculty.[21]

It is not enough that the library be well-stocked with books or even well-stocked **and** well-organized — it must be put to the test of **use** —

> Nor is it enough that the faculty be erudite professors with a thorough knowledge of their subject fields; they must make their students into educated men and women. The student comes to be guided in fields of learning by those who know the way, the faculty and the librarians, but he does not come to have his mind crammed with pre-digested ideas. If he is to receive full value from his college education, he must not only learn the facts as presented by his teachers, but he must also learn to find facts for himself from the materials which are available to him in the library. [22]

Some illustrative measures of the fourth criterion are:
(1) A library handbook (or sufficiently detailed information sheet) reaches every student as part of every registration.
(2) A LIBRARY ORIENTATION TEST FOR COLLEGE FRESHMEN [23] or a similar test is administered to all new full-time students as part of the testing program or orientation week; its results are utilized in planning library instruction and other aspects of the college program.
(3) Library orientation attendance is required of all new full-time students early in the term.
(4) A library orientation film is part of the library collection.
(5) A publication such as THE NEW LIBRARY KEY [24] is part of freshman English materials.
(6) Library instruction is fostered by library and teaching faculty in connection with specific coursework throughout the term.
(7) A library instruction course is part of the college curriculum.

5. In addition to instructional experiences, the library sponsors other non-book, library-related activities in further efforts to reach the community college student.

The community college library has a responsibility to influence students to utilize it fully and to centralize their out-of-class academic life in it. Perhaps senior colleges and universities can minimize this function and concentrate on providing course-related books. The community college has this basic responsibility and, in addition, the collection must be broadened and its students reached.

The community college library can extend itself to students primarily through library orientation and instruction but it utilizes all possible and appropriate means. Some examples are a library-audio visual club, displays, library-sponsored meetings such as an all-college film program, publication of book and reading lists, direct personal contact with students and ample directions throughout the library's facilities.

The variety of interests and abilities represented by the heterogeneous community college student body confirm the need for this varied approach. Most community colleges are attended by day students, and campus life can become decentralized and deemphasized. Lack of dormitory life and collegiate interests often leaves only the library as a potential integrative force in the student's academic life. As the ALA Standards put it:

> The junior college library is the center of curricular materials for the institution and a focal point for the cultural life on campus. . . . It furnishes reading guidance and reference service in many ways and stimulates interest in good books through displays, book lists, discussion programs etc. [25]

Some illustrative measures of the fifth criterion are:
(1)   The community college library sponsors a library-audio visual club.
(2)   It fosters library work as a career.
(3)   It provides opportunities for participation in discussion groups concerned with significant books, films and ideas.
(4)   It encourages student-purchase of books, especially paperback editions, through such activities as publicity for PAPERBOUND BOOKS IN PRINT, ETC.

6.   The library serves the community college faculty and student body as the central collection of the college's resource materials.

The expanded concept of the library as the resource center of the college — with unified purchasing, cataloging and accessibility — has proved productive and efficient in practice. An increasingly broad interpretation of library materials may include, in addition to books and such other printed publications as periodicals, pamphlets and catalogs, pictures, slides, films, phonograph records, music, tapes, filmstrips, maps, etc.

> . . . leaders in the junior college library field as well as administrators stress the fact that the library's role can be exploited by linking library practice more closely to the classroom and vice versa and by making the library a center for instructional materials of all kinds, including visual and auditory materials. [26]

All this requires quantities of well-selected library materials, with special provision for keeping the collection up-to-date — in fact, **more** books than have been considered adequate for the traditional junior college of comparable size. In general, most two-year colleges face the task of doubling their book collections to meet minimum standards and to supply needs. Intellectual work is often differentiated from recreational reading. For certain purposes and within certain limitations, this distinction has validity, but in a larger sense, personal reading may provide the intellectual framework within which the student establishes his own goals and where his tastes, aptitudes and skills find freest play.[27] The community college library has a responsibility to provide for **all** of its students' academic needs. Students must neither be forced to impose on other libraries in the community nor, as an alternative, to confine themselves to textbooks and routine work. If the library provides books related to but not required by their courses, students can broaden their viewpoints and examine their own ideas rather than rely on readymade judgments. Furthermore, when the college library becomes essentially a reserve book room, students are not given the type of educational orientation that should be provided by librarians.

Consider the case of the young person who plans to attend a local community college for two years after high school and then transfer to the state university and perhaps graduate school. He must be able to qualify for the university, and he cannot afford to lose transfer credits because of low or mediocre grades. What justification is there for his having access to an adequate library during only the second half of his college career? And later, after two years of text-book instruction, will he be able to take full advantage of adequate library facilities? His lower division years should provide equal opportunity to fulfill course requirements as well as to do supplementary work beyond basic readings and to pursue personal inquiry. As more community college students enter senior colleges, the lack of proper library facilities and advanced teaching methods in the community colleges will become apparent and can only lead to discrimination against the community college movement. Eventually also, neighboring institutions will

insist that the community college become a self-sufficient
participant in inter-library loan activities, "giving" as well
as "taking."

A minimum of 20,000 titles may seem high in view of
the meager collections of many junior college libraries, but
no instructor can expect his students to read widely if the
library collection is inadequate. Refusal to recognize and
provide for this need on the basis of its being an unrealistic
goal is one of the major causes of the community junior
college library having a role comparable to that of a high
school library.

At present not all two-year institutions possess library
buildings. In many cases, the library occupies part of the
administration or classroom building. The available space
is often far too small to permit students to do serious work
or to browse leisurely and constructively.

Some illustrative measures of the sixth criterion are:

(1) The community college library is organized as one
    coordinated collection of materials ranging in format,
    subject matter, difficulty and appeal, and is adapt-
    able by students and faculty to their instructional,
    supplemental and personal needs.

(2) The community college library collection provides
    all materials needed in the ordinary course of the
    students' work, plus related materials for depth and
    enrichment.

(3) It provides coverage in depth and extent exceeding
    the immediate requirements of the students, that is,
    sufficient to stimulate the best students and to serve
    the faculty.

(4) It contains a minimum of 20,000 titles.

(5) It has placed continuation orders for basic, standard
    reference and bibliographic-control tools; there is a
    large reference collection representing a wide range
    of difficulty and subject-matter.

(6) It contains no irrelevant materials, excessive duplica-
    tion nor obsolete books.

(7) It regularly receives, as the core of its periodical list,
    those titles indexed in READERS' GUIDE TO
    PERIODICAL LITERATURE, as well as at least
    an equal number of more specialized titles.

(8) It provides audio visual materials; there are com-

fortable facilities for previewing films and listening
to recordings.
(9) It is separately, centrally and conveniently located.
(10) It is not used as a lounge; there is provision for a
student lounge by the college.

**7. The library collection and services are appropriate for
any specialized functions of the local institution (e.g. technical programs.)**

Depending on community needs, the individual community
college may sponsor a variety of innovative curricula and
services. An example is the technical program pursued by
the terminal student in electronics, library, food and other
technologies. Materials supporting courses in these programs must be appropriate in content and at the same time,
reach the students. Monographs in engineering, for instance,
often assume an academic background in higher mathe-
matics which the technology major may not have.

Materials to support technical programs are the result
of professional book selection and coordination, faculty
recommendations, and development of planned collections.

Some illustrative measures of the seventh criterion are:
(1) The community college library collection and services
appeal to a wide range of abilities and interests.
(2) There is provision for keeping the collection up-to-
date.
(3) There is special emphasis on basic and interpretive
works.
(4) Instructional films related to technology programs
are purchased on a continuing basis.

**8. The library collection and services are appropriate for
any non-curricular learning experiences of the local institution (e.g. vocational guidance.)**

Another area in which the community college library
program, if it is to be effective, should do more than the
four-year college is in its relationship with students. Because of the great variety of aptitudes, interests, skills and
experiences of the students, librarians assume positions of
increasing importance in guidance. They may act as counselors for those who need direction in how to study and for
superior students who can profit from an amplified program

of study. The work of the readers' advisor and the readers' advisory services becomes increasingly important to the community college library program.

Librarians can cooperate in community college guidance services by encouraging personal investigation and broad reading interests, fostering good work habits and skills in the use of materials, providing books and other information to help students meet the problems of adolescence and maturity, stimulating the exploration of occupational information, and by working with honors students as well as with reading improvement classes.

Some illustrative measures of the eighth criterion are:

(1) Community college library collections and services provide for cultural breadth as well as practical competence.

(2) They emphasize fiction and biography in addition to the traditional nonfiction areas.

(3) They include vocational materials, as a major evidence of involvement in the guidance program.

(4) They include a comprehensive college catalog collection.

(5) They provide help for the slower student in how to improve reading and study skills.

(6) There is a comfortable and appealing browsing area featuring new books.

9. Arrangement and servicing of materials facilitate their use by community college students and faculty.

No matter how well selected and extensive its collection, the value of any college library is diminished if its materials are not arranged and serviced to facilitate their fullest use. The variety of format and content needed in the community college library collection intensifies the need for accessibility.

Arrangement and servicing of materials to facilitate their use are, however, basically dependent upon the organizational ability of the library director and the staff and funds available to him. Some of the means of meeting this criterion are based on proven college library administrative practice while others are unique to the community college.

Some illustrative measures of the ninth criterion are:

(1) There is a simplified and logical arrangement of materials.

(2) There is an open stack area.

(3) There is an ample supply of reserve materials to meet special needs.

(4) There is seating for at least 25% of the full-time enrollment.

(5) There is an up-to-date card catalog with entries for materials on order, ample subject guides, analytics and cross-references.

(6) The library is able to be open to its public for as many hours as are needed to fulfill the functions of the local community college program.

(7) Order and quiet are commensurate with efficient and comfortable library use.

10. The library is administered efficiently and effectively within the policies of the local community college.

The successful community college library program is inevitably built around people, and the key person in this complex is the library director. One researcher has found "the highest possible correlation between the training and personality of the librarian (i.e. library director) and the efficiency of the library" and little correlation between the age of the school and the size of the book collection.[28]

The library director makes contact with every person connected with the community college and at the same time administers a program, budget and staff of his own. It is he who sets up, develops and modifies systems and routines. He deals with people, monies, goals and realities.

In the well-administered college today . . . the librarian is selected with care, for he must be an active and effective participant in administration, curriculum building, program operation, evaluation, and further planning . . .

The administrator who takes advantage of the opportunity not only provides adequate facilities, budget, and staff, but typically he also:

1. makes the position of librarian one of major importance on the instructional staff,

2. makes the library the resource center of instructional materials — including not only books, magazines, and

other printed materials, but also motion pictures, recordings, slides, filmstrips, and other audio visual
materials,

3. uses the library as an avenue of instructional supervision,

4. recognizes the role of the library in educational
engineering.[29]

When there is lack of an established college policy for
library administration, vacillation in aims and, consequently, in achievement occur. Optimum understanding between
the president as chief administrative officer and the library
director facilitates attainment of both all-college and library
objectives. Library administration should be related to
college administration and the library director's function
clearly established within the administration and organization of the institution. A statement, reviewed from time to
time, of the library director's authority and responsibilities
as the administrator sees them would guide and facilitate
realization of objectives and make them more purposeful.
It should be clear that the library director is in charge of
his organization and has control of his budget, personnel
and book selection. Responsibility to define formal channels
of communication and the extent of authority and personal
support originates with the administrator. The important
part the community college administrator plays is pointed
up by Branscomb's statement that

. . . ultimately the college president is responsible for
the conduct and character of the library. If he would
secure the fullest educational returns from his college
library, there are three specific services which he must
render it, besides providing adequate financial support.
These are

(a) to take the lead in clarifying in the minds of all
concerned the kind of library program which the college
wants,

(b)   to select the librarian qualified to direct that service,
and

(c) to see to it that in the organization of the college the
librarian is not separated from, but rather is brought

into vital relationship to, the educational program. In most colleges this will mean elevating the status of the librarian (i.e. library director).[30]

One study of the administrative relationships of the library and the junior college concludes that the president as chief administrative officer should appoint the library director, establish his faculty and administrative status, include him on committees concerning administrative and institutional policy, establish channels of communication between his office and the library, and keep the library director informed of all plans and policies of the administration and institution. The library director should be directly responsible to the president, prepare an annual report for him, have responsibility for the library budget, have responsibility for library materials, and keep the president informed of all changes in library policy and services, addition of materials and staff needs.[31]

Effective administrative organization should provide for a limited span of control for all officials. It should also provide for the delegation of authority commensurate with responsibility. If the library director is considered a major administrative officer, he will be responsible to the chief administrative officer. The college library is an organization in itself — with its own operational budget and relationship with every aspect of the college program and a director who serves as a member of both line and staff personnel.

Until recently the librarian was, as a rule, directly responsible to the president. In an increasing number of colleges and universities today, the librarian is made responsible to the president through an academic vice president or dean. This change has come about as a result of recent efforts at reorganization . . . in line with the span of control principle that there should be only a small number of major administrative officers reporting directly to the president. It places the librarian at a disadvantage in presenting the needs of a developing library program . . .[32]

In order to support its unique institution's functions the community college library usually surpasses its collegiate counterpart in supply of course-related books, and especially

in personnel and services. Responsibility to an academic
dean or dean of instruction can be inadequate and time-
consuming when applied to community college library
directorship.
A number of variables may influence the decision. One
is personnel currently employed. There may be an academic
vice president who is exceptionally well-informed about
library matters and who has the educational vision and
authority to give the library strong support. On the other
hand, new or small community colleges may not have
personnel in these posts, just as the library director may
well be the only librarian on the faculty. Where the community college is part of a school system or district, the
organization may be structured by the board of education
or other official body. Thus the size of the institution and
the kind of control can also effect the relationship of the
library director to college administration. The decision as
to whom the library director reports is often made by the
community college president. He may recognize a need to
structure his administration so that the library director
reports directly to him, and the library program thereby
takes on greater significance in the total college program.
What is sought here is a sympathetic interest and strong
support for the library on the part of the community college
chief administrator. The local situation should therefore be
studied by him with reference to establishing a relationship
between the library director and administration which facilitates the management, growth and development of the library
program.
Some administrators say that librarians fail to demonstrate the need for funds and that minimum percentages
which librarians may advocate are arbitrary. Such officers
discount statistics, standards and the fact that a library
program, while part of the college program, is a total operation in itself. This may be due in part to the fact that the
administrator's background has more likely been in the
classroom than in the library. It is particularly unfortunate
in the community college, because so many are new institutions whose library programs require extra support initially,
and whose needs should be based on an assumption rather
than on continued demonstration or defense.
A college library program requires capital funding at

the outset and a regular, annual percent of college funds for maintenance. From time to time, additional special allocations are needed, for in addition to reflecting all of the college's expansions and changes, the library also feels the effects of such things as the explosion of knowledge, teacher-training methods and secondary school library programing. The regular college library maintenance budget should therefore represent a stable minimum percent of the total college funds. This has been found to be one of the best ways of assuring support of an optimum rather than a token library program.

The college library program outlined in the ALA junior college standards normally requires a minimum of 5% of the total educational and general college budget. This minimum percentage is for a well established library program with an adequate collection, and it does not include audio visual. (The library budget for a newly organized junior college, for an older junior college whose library holdings are seriously deficient, where there is rapid expansion in student population or course offerings, or where the institution sponsors a wide range of studies and activities — such as the community college does — should, logically, be greater.) The 5% minimum maintenance budget is based on the consensus of many junior college librarians consulted as well as on an analysis of junior college library statistics made available to the committee preparing the Standards. When library budgets sink below the median ratio of library expenditures to total education and general institutional expenditures for comparable institutions as indicated in the latest college library statistics, there is almost always confirmation of the validity of this allotment. It has been suggested that if the recommended minimum were reached by all junior colleges not now spending 5% of their college budgets on their libraries' maintenance, "the dollars let loose for library purposes would revolutionize holdings, staffs and services."[33]

In the final analysis, it is the allocation of adequate funds (assuming attention has been given promptly to filling the position of library director with a well-qualified person) — in the planning stage as well as the continued development program — that indicates the founders' and administration's sincere support and knowledge of the

community college library. True, the library director must
utilize his budget in such a way as to prove his program,
demonstrate its vital importance to the community college
and extend its scope, but inadequate funds make him little
more than a keeper-of-books struggling to clear his desk
each day. "The president's responsibility for the progress
as well as the character of the college library is ultimate."[34]

The community college library and its program influences
every student and instructor, every instructional program
and the fulfillment of every other type of community college
activity and function. The close tie is responsible for a new
relationship between the library and people involved in
every aspect of college life. The time has come to discard
the concept of the library needing "a librarian," anymore
than the English department's needs consist of "an English
teacher." Professional librarians are needed in the positions
of library director and head of each library area, depending
on the size of the institution and how the library director
structures his program, e.g. circulation, audio visual,
readers' advisory and instruction, acquisitions and cataloging. Johnson deplores the fact that,

> . . . At times in the past administrators have used library
> positions as posts to which to relegate faculty misfits.
> . . . Or, perhaps the library staff was assembled from
> recent library school graduates with full knowledge of
> library techniques but with as yet undeveloped concepts
> of the place of the library in curriculum building.[35]

In addition to the basic graduate library degree, some
coursework in education, particularly the community college, non-book materials and curriculum are needed by
the library director and desirable for all of the professional
library staff. Suitable experience must be sought in the
background of the library director, for without successful
administrative experience, the well-trained librarian is as
unprepared for college library direction as the medical
school graduate without his internship would be for independent practice.

A library committee is no substitute for a professional
library director. The functions of a library committee are
"advisory and informative, not administrative or executive."
Administration by a faculty committee is "sure to be slow,

is likely to be vacillating and in the last analysis is lacking in responsibility." Experience has shown repeatedly that the only satisfactory way to administer the college library is to place authority in the librarian and set up for him contacts with the faculty which will be both natural and official. [36]

Basic to the efficient administration of the community college library is a well thought-out book policy, continuously reviewed and flexible. Although book selection is in the library director's domain, he must strive for administrative support and faculty understanding of the policy. Recommendations from the entire professional library staff and from the college faculty should be encouraged and followed up as much as possible, but the library director is the person in a position to see and relate the total picture. Channeling of requests for book purchases correlated with instruction through the departmental chairman to the library director serves several purposes. The procedure may influence instructors to make more judicious selections. It can keep the chairman alert as to library use by his department and the extent of funds going for materials in his subject area(s). And it tends to bring the library director and other departmental chairmen into closer working contact.

Some illustrative measures of the tenth criterion are:

(1) The library director has knowledge of and enthusiasm about the community college movement.

(2) The library director reports to the college president (chief administrative officer) and is responsible for preparation and administration of the library budget.

(3) The library director is a member of various college committees, especially curriculum.

(4) The library director has ultimate responsibility for book selection; he/she solicits, encourages and acts promptly upon recommendations from the entire college staff.

(5) Each member of the community college professional library staff as a minimum holds the fifth-year degree in library service.

(6) Professional librarians assume the same responsibility for student morale and welfare as do other faculty.

(7) There are at least two professional librarians on the community college library staff, with an additional librarian and clerk for each 1,000 full-time enrollment over 2,000. (There is an additional professional librarian if centralized or commercial book cataloging and processing are not available.)

(8) There are at least two staff members, one of whom is a professional librarian, on duty at all times that the library is open to the public; student workers are never alone on duty in the library nor at the circulation desk.

(9) The library maintenance budget is at least 5% of the budget of the well-established community college; before first classes and during the first five years, more funds are needed.

(10) The library director is qualified by experience as well as training, and he is recruited early in the development of the new community college.

Chapter III

CURRENT COMMUNITY COLLEGE
LIBRARY PRACTICE

It is useful to evaluate current community college library
practice reported in the questionnaire by means of the
previously established criteria. The criteria have been employed to analyze the questionnaire data and the comments
of the library directors because they are flexible and func-
tional tests of the degree of adequacy of a community
college's program, or parts of the program, and because
they have been constructed to apply specifically to the
community college library. Examination of the questionnaire data has been made with reference to the illustrative
measures evolved for the individual criterion, as well as
other questionnaire data relevant to its demonstration in
the one hundred three reporting community college libraries.
These data have usually provided varying degrees of positive and negative evidence of demonstration of the criterion,
as well as helpful details of the picture of current practice.
The analysis has therefore required considerable interpretation and discussion of current practice related to each
criterion. It has been useful to keep part of Good's description of evaluation in mind. (Evaluation is)

> Consideration of evidence in light of value standards
> and in terms of the particular situation and the goals
> which the group or individual is striving to attain.
> . . . the process of ascertaining or judging value or
> amount of something by careful appraisal . . . [37]

1. The over-all library program reflects the curriculum, objectives and functions of the local community college.

Analysis of questionnaire data and statements of the library directors relevant to the first criterion provide evidence that current, well-established library programs reflect the curriculum, objectives and functions of the local community colleges to a great degree. At the same time, however, many library directors consider that their programs could and should support their institutions' functions to a greater degree. (A complete report of the questionnaire appears in the Appendix. A summary of data relevant to the first criterion follows this section.)

Lack of consideration for the library in the planning of new community colleges is a factor which has inhibited supportive library programs. There is often evidence of a great lack of consideration for the library in planning new community colleges: for example, library provision may consist of an allocation of one room and uncoordinated book selection by faculty until the library director is brought in belatedly. Or, the library building which is included in the new campus plan is among the first to be delayed when deadlines and finances must be adjusted. Or, there is failure to employ a qualified library director at least a year before first classes. Placement counsellors of graduate schools of library service and education attest to the facts that all possible resources to obtain such personnel are not fully utilized and that the prospective employer often over-emphasizes the requirement for a male library director, while de-emphasizing the need for appropriate experience.

Current cooperative library planning by community college faculty, administration, students and interested laymen exists in a variety of forms, most frequently a library committee. Statements of the library directors suggest, however, that this is frequently the result of administrative appointment of faculty eager to evaluate books but who rarely attend meetings and do little to influence their students librarywise. Library directors feel no need for such a community college library committee where there is an active, all-college committee on which they serve. These are usually planning committees consisting of departmental representatives having administrative status.

An on-going approach is well-evidenced by a variety of procedural innovations, although some library directors prefer not to specify innovations but, rather, to draw attention to the fact that their philosophy is one of continued growth. Innovations and modifications in the library programs are most frequent in the areas of building improvements and increase in library hours. Others include the acquisition of periodicals on microfilm, introduction of library orientation, audio visual improvement and acquisition or selling of paperbacks.

Judgment of the data by application of the first criterion leads to the conclusion that the library programs of the reporting community colleges reflect their institutions' current curricula, objectives and functions. Study of the data relevant to other criteria also supports this reaction in the areas of collection and services. Illustration of such a broad criterion appears or fails to appear in **all** aspects of the program. **But** the job could be sooner and better done. A minimum of a year's preplanning, coupled with the immediate appointment of a capable library director and the provision of an adequate budget, are the conditions needed for basic library programing. They are generally lacking in the reporting community colleges.

Summary of the questionnaire data relevant to the first criterion:

93.2% of the community college library programs are cooperatively planned to some extent by community college faculty, students and interested laymen;

72.8% reflect an on-going approach, as evidenced by the existence of procedural innovations;

68.9% have library committees;

the library director is chairman of less than half of the library committees;

the stated function of less than half of the library committees is "advisory;" of one third, it is not defined;

12.6% of the community college library programs resulted from planning begun at least one year before first classes were enrolled;

there are no written reports of library surveys on which

library programs of new community colleges were based; and

more than half of those community colleges which are more than five years old have added fewer than 10,000 volumes in their first five years.

II. There is provision for continuous evaluation of the community college library program by means of appropriate techniques and measures.

Analysis of questionnaire data relevant to the second criterion shows consistent enthusiasm for the recent ALA Standards. However, they are utilized mainly by library directors, who describe college administrators as lacking in acquaintance with or appreciation of the Standards. Recognition of the utility of the ALA Standards by the library directors is significant, for it means that there is some provision for continuous evaluation of most community college library programs by means of appropriate techniques and measures.

Statements by the library directors reveal mixed reactions as to the application of the Standards, however. For example,

The criticisms made by the AAJC Commission on Administration reveal an alarming lack of knowledge of college library functions and confusion with high school on the part of the presidents and administrators.

Pressure on governing boards and administrators from outside the college is needed to raise library standards.

Librarians try to get the Standards over to administration and get nowhere until much later, (accreditation) recommendations are along more or less the same lines.

The problem is to get administrative support; . . . they consider state and regional standards . . . I wish state, regional, junior college associations would adopt them (i.e., the ALA Standards).

Minimum standards are useful only when they are interpreted as general guidelines for the resources needed to meet the minimum needs of an average institution — specialized curricula demand far more library materials.

A capable librarian and an ALA Standard-budget are all that are needed.

Until the library directors are able to communicate to their chief administrators their belief in the value of the ALA Standards, the funds necessary for implementation will not be forthcoming. The fact that accrediting bodies ultimately make recommendations along similar lines does not diminish the alarming implications of the situation, for the ALA Standards are basically planning guidelines, whereas accrediting recommendations are commentaries on existing inadequacies.

Current library programs are not often evaluated by means of the professional library survey, possibly because this usually involves an expenditure for the service itself and the implementation of recommendations. In the long run, recommendations which are implemented are those made by college accrediting or supervisory agencies, 60.1% of the library programs having received specific recommendations. Accrediting and supervisory agencies' most frequent recommendations are: increased library facilities, especially seating; increased library staff, especially librarians; increased collection, referring to quantity rather than quality; increased library budget, and increased library use by faculty.

There is provision for continuous evaluation by appropriate techniques by the library directors, but lack of funds or authority with which to implement change indicated by evaluative techniques is also indicated in the questionnaire data and the respondents' comments.

Summary of the questionnaire data relevant to the second criterion:

guidelines for evaluation provided by the ALA Standards are utilized by 78.6% of the reporting library directors;

a library consultant was employed in the preplanning of only five (4.8%) of the community colleges;

19.4% of the current library programs have been evaluated by a professional consultant whose survey recommendations are not always implemented;

specific recommendations of accrediting or supervisory

agencies have been made concerning 60.1% of the library programs and are usually being carried out;

28.1% of the community college libraries have no workroom facilities whatsoever; 47.5% have only one room for use by the public.

III. Within the limits of its resources and responsibilities, the community college library facilitates the research work and professional growth of the faculty.

Application of the measures as well as other evidence indicate that plans and efforts to facilitate the research work and professional growth of community college faculty exist in good number, but that shortages of staff and materials limit the best of intentions. Respondents recognize the need for and attempt to provide a variety of materials related to faculty interests and specialties, as well as services which will facilitate and expedite their utilization.

Data and statements throughout the questionnaires point to three main areas of inadequacies in current community college library programing (seating, quantities of books and staffing), two of which — shortages of staff and materials — would seem restrictive upon fulfillment of plans and goals related to the third criterion. For example, when it is necessary for a library director to make a choice of expenditure among various materials, application of the third criterion might well require diversion of limited funds from curriculum-related books needed for student reserves to specialized journals requested by one faculty member.

Attention was drawn by library directors to faculty interpretation of library service for them often amounting to "covering" for deficient library and professional backgrounds and prompt purchase of materials requested by them for their personal use. The materials requested by them generally do not include such subject matter as the community college, audio visual methods, guidance and curriculum. The library directors' comments include,

> The faculty members do not make periodic and thorough checks of their areas.

> Stimulating faculty use (and thereby student use also) of the library and its facilities (is a problem).

Many faculty members tend to stay with the landmark books of their subject-matters for years; they are still recommending and using titles which were outstanding when they were undergraduates — even in science.

If every faculty member could have a conference with a librarian each semester to discuss use made and to be made in his area of reserves, for instance, (it would be ideal).

Summary of the questionnaire data relevant to the third criterion:

79.6% of the community college libraries provide teachers' materials in subject areas as well as in education, audio visual and community college fields;

all but three (2.9%) subscribe to THE JUNIOR COLLEGE JOURNAL; 89.3% have some back files on hand;

80.5% are involved in inter-library cooperation;

93.2% distribute news bulletins and booklists as a routine procedure;

faculty book recommendations are expedited: — acquisition of duplicate copies, textbooks, out-of-print books, and paperback editions, and establishment of reserve collections is typically based on instructor-request;

66% of inter-library activities are in behalf of the faculty; and

66% of the teachers' materials collections are utilized only occasionally.

IV. Instructional experiences in library usage are provided as needed by the community college student body.

Library orientation, instruction and technology are distinctive parts of current community college library practice.

Library orientation usually refers to an introductory experience provided for new students at the beginning of each term. About one third of the community colleges attempt to accomplish this as part of freshman English class by means of a "unit" in the textbook "covering" the library, which often amounts to a classroom assignment to "read

the section on the library." The report that library orientation attendance is required of all new full-time students early
in the term by more than half of the community colleges is
misleading, since few library directors consider this provision adequate — probably due to the fact that typically
it consists of either the "unit" in freshman English or a
necessarily hasty tour of the library.

Some sort of library orientation as part of a freshman
week orientation program is provided by 10.6% of the
community colleges. Respondents report that orientation does
not generally utilize testing devices, nor is it a genuine
orientation to an important aspect of community college
life. Library orientation may, however, consist of half a
day and include the library tour (getting to know the staff,
facilities and feeling of the library) and a class in elementary
utilization of some basic references, bibliographies and indexes and the card catalog. Library orientation as part
of a semester-long freshman orientation course, during
which the librarian is able to utilize several class meetings,
presenting the library tour plus some instruction to provide
at least minimal experiences needed for acquaintance with
the card catalog and basic reference and bibliographic tools
is provided by 11.6%. Replies which consider orientation
provision adequate tend to originate in community colleges
in which it is part of such a required freshman orientation
course. Library orientation is raised in status, more time
allocated to it, and the librarian enabled to do an adequate
job in a combined classroom-library situation.

Library instruction may consist of visits to a class by
a librarian, upon teacher-request, for instruction in the
use of the library's resources in the aspect of the subject
currently being studied. It may also consist of the more
formal, scheduled course meeting, typically, once a week
for one elective credit.

A library instruction course is part of the course offerings
of 18.4% of the community colleges; in some it is a strong
future possibility, and it has been discontinued for lack of
staff in others. It usually develops to meet the needs of
students whose pre-college library experiences have been
inadequate and in community colleges which have recognized that there must be upgrading of current library provision if transfer to senior colleges is to be made with

equality. This provision, of course, only partially fills the gap, as the basic differences are in quantity and quality of book collections and professional library service. There is a strong feeling that the nature of the community college student and the impossibility of providing adequate library orientation are such that a course should be required of all new full-time students. For instance,

The nature of the community college student requires that there be supervision.

Our student body is not prepared to use any library.

First, I would like to incorporate a library instruction course for all freshmen, with some credit attached to it, to inform students how to use the information at their fingertips.

Library technology refers to the recent community college development in the training of clerical library personnel. It is, therefore, a curriculum in itself and may consist of a sequence of technical courses integrated with the college requirements in general education and lead to one of the junior college associate degrees. (In general, the professional librarian's training consists of a BA in liberal arts and a Master's degree from an accredited library school, to prepare him to satisfy state and local certification requirements as well as to acquire experience leading to administrative and teaching responsibility.) Four (3.8%) of the community colleges report library technology curricula. Others indicate strong interest.

At present such programs are offered as "Vocational Library Clerk" in California. One reply (from California) typifies the opposing view: "not collegiate." It fails to recognize that adequate staffing of all types of libraries includes various kinds as well as numbers of personnel. In New York State, library technology has been tried experimentally in the community college and discontinued. Its success seems to depend on community needs, attitudes and personnel to implement such programs, as well as legal provisions which will prevent the placement of library technology "graduates" in positions for which they are not qualified.

Summary of the questionnaire data relevant to the fourth criterion:

> instruction is fostered in connection with coursework by 66.9% of the community college library programs;

> a library handbook reaches every student during registration in 42.7% of the reporting community colleges;

> a library orientation test is administered to all new full-time students of 14.5% of the colleges;

> library orientation attendance is required of all new full-time students early in the term of 56.3% of the community colleges;

> fifty-five of the fifty-eight library directors reporting required library orientation consider it inadequate;

> a library orientation film is part of the collections of six (5.8%) of the community college libraries;

> a publication such as THE NEW LIBRARY KEY is part of freshman English materials in 13.5% of the community colleges;

> a library instruction course is part of the college offerings of 18.4%;

> library instruction is provided in a pre-vocational curriculum of four community colleges;

> little or no efforts, aside from reserves, are made by instructors to integrate library use and coursework in 51.4% of the community colleges; and

> "some efforts" to encourage general reading are made by instructors in 37.8% of the colleges.

V. In addition to instructional experiences, the library sponsors other non-book, library-related activities in further efforts to reach the community college student.

Recognition of the responsibility to influence students to utilize the community college library fully and to centralize much of their out-of-class life in it is apparent in the statements of library directors:

> The greatest problem area to me is student attendance in the library: our students do not stay on campus

after class and consequently, do not make the use that could be made of the library resources which exist.

Have the library take over the leadership in the development and presentation of cultural events on campus, e.g. lectures, book talks, private-library contests, etc.

. . . impossible in the present set-up; (we will be able to) in our new building.

How can students be stimulated to a consistent program of extra-curricular reading?

Our evening opening is largely nullified for hundreds of students who live great distances from the community college in such a large territory.

But full implementation of this criterion seems to be delayed where local needs require that priority be given to the activities related to the fourth criterion, library instruction. The data indicating that only about one quarter of the libraries provide opportunities for participation in discussion groups must be examined closely because almost all of the others regret that it is impossible "in the present set up", that is — the college is old and the library crowded, or the college is new and the collection inadequate.

About one quarter of the community college library programs encourage student-purchase of books through a variety of means. The problem is lack of staff time, so that this practice is reported by newer community colleges with their own library buildings, at least two professional librarians and collections verging on adequacy. Reasons given for the lack or failure of a library-audio visual club are that it is "not considered collegiate" or that the college program is "already too full to support another activity." Both reasons may be related to the library club as a traditional high school activity.

Merely providing and maintaining facilities in which students can sit, write and refer to a small collection consume the staff and financial resources of many community college libraries. Even the libraries with adequate book budgets may lack adequate seating or stack space, and the activities related to this criterion for the most part require space.

Summary of the questionnaire data relevant to the fifth criterion:

library work is fostered by 62.1% of the library programs of the reporting community colleges;

there is one community college library-audio visual club;

comfortable facilities for previewing films and listening to recordings are provided by 33.9% of the community colleges;

27.1% of the community college libraries are able to provide opportunities for students to participate in discussion groups concerned with significant books, films and ideas;

11.6% of the community colleges are members of film libraries, pools or other centralized groups; and

30% of the community college libraries encourage student purchase of books, especially paperback editions.

VI. The library serves the community college faculty and student body as the central collection of the college's resource materials.

Community college library collections contain a variety of materials; the majority of the collections are made up of books, films, filmstrips, slides, recordings, periodicals and pamphlets, with additional items of microfilm, maps and globes, paintings and prints, government documents, programs, transparencies, tapes, clippings, charts and plates well represented. Several library directors dislike the term, "instructional materials center." They point out that to effectively support the community college program, the library must be a provider of much more than course-related materials, the philosophy inherent in several of the criteria.

While about one third of the reporting libraries have programs responsible for their college audio visual materials and services, approximately the same number have no such responsibility, and information from the balance was insufficient to reach a conclusion regarding audio visual arrangements. It should be noted, however, that 11.6% of the community colleges participate in film pools or other cooperative arrangements which are generally popular and effective.

With less than half of the reporting libraries able to provide all materials needed in the course of their students'
work, it follows that the average students need to utilize
other libraries, but whether they do so is doubtful. When
it is financially possible to provide some coverage in depth
and extent exceeding immediate requirements of the students,
professional techniques and approaches are routinely and
amply utilized.

There is other evidence that libraries do not stimulate
the best students and serve faculty sufficiently: less than
20,000 volumes, a curriculum-weighted collection, simply
not having the book when needed, collection and budget
remaining static while enrollment (and budget recommendations) increase, interloan and permission to use other libraries requested too often, and most serious of all — the
need to limit books loaned.

Only 36.8% of the libraries contain a minimum of 20,000
volumes. A closer look at these data reveals that five of
the community colleges are unable to have 20,000 volumes
even as a goal because of lack of space, and that 27.1%
have less than 10,000 volumes. (And 20,000 titles should
be the real goal.) A recent editorial in the education section
of the NEW YORK TIMES confirms these findings and
their significance.

> Two basic facts emerge from all recent studies: there
> are not nearly enough books available in school and
> college libraries; and the pressure on the public libraries,
> as a result of these shortages, is reaching the crisis stage.

> All these issues are coming to a head for a vital reason.
> As nation-wide school reforms move into high gear,
> the stress on independent study has moved the book —
> not just the textbook — into the center of the educational
> stage. [38]

About one quarter of the libraries are not centrally or
conveniently located, and have no separate workroom. More
than one third are shared with another institution, usually
a high school. Reports are consistently accompanied by
descriptions of the inadvisability of this type of arrangement. For example,

> The community college should have its own campus

42 COMMUNITY COLLEGE LIBRARY

and own library, and not just be 'more high school.'
Unless it has its own campus . . . and maintains regular college standards, with . . . a faculty that is geared
to college teaching, it will just be a continuation of
high school.

The abilities and reading interests of high school and
junior college students especially are too far apart to
be compatible.

About half of the community colleges do not have separate
library buildings and have only one library room for use
by the public.

It may be that the typical community college library is
organized as one collection because it is a scant collection,
allocated to a limited area within another building and
regarded much as a high school library. Where there is
need to utilize other libraries — in locales where others are
accessible — it seems doubtful that students follow through.
It is more likely that they utilize textbook and encyclopedia,
if the instructor condones this pattern. 91.2% of the community college libraries function as central collections of all
of the college's resource materials, but these collections are
shockingly inadequate.

**Summary of the questionnaire data relevant to the sixth
criterion:**

the libraries of 91.2% of the community colleges are
organized as one coordinated collection of materials
ranging in format, subject matter, difficulty and appeal;

18.4% of the community colleges have departmental,
divisional or collections other than the central library;

some coverage in depth and extent exceeding the immediate requirements of the students (that is, sufficient
to stimulate the best students and to serve the faculty)
is provided by 57.2% of the libraries;

practically all of the responding library directors regard
as standard library procedure such things as placement
of continuation orders for basic, standard reference and
bibliographic-control tools, a large reference collection
representing a wide range of difficulty, elimination of
irrelevant, excessively-duplicated and obsolete materials,

and regular receipt of almost all of the titles indexed in READERS' GUIDE TO PERIODICAL LITERATURE;

74.7% of the community college libraries are centrally and conveniently located;

84.8% of the community colleges provide some separate student lounge facilities;

66% of the libraries are considered instructional materials centers;

40.7% provide all library resource materials needed in the ordinary course of the students' work;

67.9% of the average students need to use other libraries occasionally;

34.9% of the community colleges are close to a public library or public library branch, i.e. within walking distance or less than one mile (but 55.3% of the colleges are located in urban areas and 12% in rural);

36.8% of the collections contain at least 20,000 volumes (27.1% have less than 10,000 volumes);

37.8% of the library programs provide their institutions' audio visual materials and services;

52.4% of the community college libraries are housed in separate buildings; and

37.8% of the community college libraries are shared with the libraries of other institutions; the library directors of 54% of these community colleges consider the arrangements "unacceptable."

VII. The library collection and services are appropriate for any specialized functions of the local institution (e.g. technical programs.)

It can be said that the library collections and services are appropriate for specialized functions of about half of the community colleges. It is true of the balance only insofar as there is financial provision to make possible implementation of the techniques — mainly professional book selection — which exist and which are known to the responding library directors. Specialized community college functions which the library is most frequently called upon to support

are the technical programs. Consideration for the wide
range of abilities and interests of community college students
goes hand in hand with this assignment. There is evidence
of awareness of these responsibilities in the statements of
the library directors' goals and problems. For example,

> Just what should a junior college library contain — how
> much top-level high school materials, how much scholar-
> ly upper-class and reserve material? Should it be cata-
> loged simply or with a university library's precision in
> classifying? How much good textbook material should
> it accept for reserve use, and should all old editions
> be discarded?

> The next problem is getting proper use of library ma-
> terials from a freshman-sophomore clientele who have
> enough trouble getting through the textbook, much less
> reading something from the library . . .

> (We should have) regional workshops in reference and
> other library techniques for upgrading and refreshing
> library personnel . . .

> (We should aim) to make the library an integral part
> of the instructional program. This will probably require
> some reorganization of instructional methods — less
> reliance on lecture, more on individual study, less
> rigidity in class and assignment scheduling . . .

> (We should have) five years' unbound periodicals circu-
> lating from supervised open shelves; microcards of older
> periodicals needing to be circulated, with inexpensive
> hand readers . . .

> Introduction of vocational library clerk program on
> an academic basis as another terminal vocational course
> (is a goal).

Lack of funds with which to purchase, process and intro-
duce quantities of materials curtails such plans. There can,
for instance, be little or no acquisition of instructional films
related to technical programs without budgetary provision
for the films as well as for the costs their processing and
use imply. In the meantime, professional book selection is
the principal means to the fulfillment of this criterion.

Individual approaches evolved under pressure to fill local

needs were often reported. But attempts to set up exchange relationships, for instance, are not possible for many community colleges, as they lack the assets with which to "barter." Time consumed soliciting gifts is generally agreed to be costly, and cataloging short-cuts often lead to the neglect of books which are not consistently or thoroughly represented in the card catalog or on the shelf.

Summary of the questionnaire data relevant to the seventh criterion:

there is special provision for keeping the collection up-to-date in 71.8% of the community college library programs;

approximately half of the community college library collections appeal to a wide range of abilities and interests; there is special emphasis on basic and interpretive works, as demonstrated by such facts as 63.1% having materials representing a variety of format, 57.2% providing "some coverage" in depth and extent exceeding immediate requirements of the students, and 63.1% utilizing standard basic bibliographies in book selection;

there is little emphasis on the acquisition of instructional films related to technical programs, i.e. they are not purchased on a continuing basis;

10.6% of the majority of students need to use other libraries extensively; and

very few of the community college libraries have placed continuation orders for such technical abstract/index tools as APPLIED SCIENCE & TECHNOLOGY INDEX, BUSINESS PERIODICALS INDEX, BIOLOGICAL ABSTRACTS, CHEM ABSTRACTS, INDEX MEDICUS, TECHNICAL BOOK REVIEW INDEX, ENGINEERING INDEX. It follows that the periodicals, journals and books indexed in these sources will not be in the collections of the libraries.

VIII. The library collection and services are appropriate for any non-curricular learning experiences of the local institution (e.g. vocational guidance.)

In several respects, Criteria 7 and 8 are companions —

seven relating to library support for specialized functions,
such as technical programs, and eight to non-curricular
learning experiences, such as vocational guidance, of the
local institution.

The data portray the majority of community college
library programs providing for personal development as
well as practical competence of their student communities
in the several ways listed in the data summary — for instance, emphasizing fiction and biography as well as the
traditional non-fiction areas; providing vocational materials, comprehensive college catalog collections, practically
all of the periodical titles indexed in READERS' GUIDE
TO PERIODICAL LITERATURE; facilitating discussion
groups and fostering library work as a career.

One of the main techniques advocated by all of the library
directors in order to provide collections and services appropriate to curricular as well as non-curricular community
college learning experiences has yet to be implemented.
**Only two libraries are able to provide continuous profes-
sional readers' advisory service.** In view of many community college students' inexperience in using library
resources and in independent thinking, this is probably
the most serious personnel lack aside from library directorship.

**Summary of the questionnaire data relevant to the eighth
criterion:**

89.3% of the community college libraries emphasize
fiction and biography in addition to the traditional
non-fiction areas:

88.3% include vocational materials as a major evidence
of involvement in the guidance program, but several
library directors refer to disorganized vocational materials collections in the counseling centers as deterrents
to the effectiveness of the library program;

65% include a comprehensive college catalog collection;

about half of the community college library collections
and services provide for cultural breadth as well as
practical competence, as demonstrated by such facts
as 54.3% receiving 1-5 periodical titles in foreign
languages regularly, 27.1% facilitating participation in

discussion groups, 62.1% fostering library work as a career, 30% encouraging student-purchase of books, and 37.8% of the library directors considering that "some efforts" other than placing books on reserve are made by instructors to encourage general reading;

43.6% provide help for the slower student in reading improvement and study skills;

there are comfortable and appealing browsing areas featuring new books in 45.6% of the responding libraries; many browsing areas have had to be given up to such basics as additional stacks and table space; and

two libraries are able to provide a professional readers' advisory service.

IX. Arrangement and servicing of materials facilitate their use by community college students and faculty.

Efforts to arrange and service materials to facilitate their use by students and faculty have been made in all of the responding community college libraries. Almost all of the libraries utilize open stacks to bring books and students closer, although they have found that this policy can foster stealing where there are insufficient supervisory staff and inefficiency resulting from the need to use quarters not designed for library use, as is often the case in community colleges. New library buildings are able to utilize such techniques as the controlled single exit. They are open long hours. Reserve collections are provided. Central collections of resource materials are the rule. Cataloging is generally up-to-date. Simplified arrangements of materials and innovative techniques are sought.

The more articulate library directors declare that experience has led them to conclude that, where the library collection is adequate and library use is fostered by teachers and library staff, reserve collections should be de-emphasized in favor of subject assignments, reading lists, broad general reading and stack use, possibly in combination with required, mass readings from purchased (paperback) books. They feel it is impossible to provide "ample collections of reserve materials" (the wording used in the questionnaire.) Reserve collections which consist of multiple copies of mass textual reading assignments often gulped down at the last

minute foster little learning, independent thinking, originality
or creativity on the part of the student; the library directors
refer to their fostering theft and mutilation on this part of
the collection and neglect of the balance. Some of their
comments include:

> (A problem) is the instructor who gives required read-
> ings and informs the library after the class. It's the same
> story everywhere, I know, **but** there are more part-time
> faculty in the community college.

> Materials seem no particular problem if enough budget
> is available.

> (Reserves) should be only one of several reading en-
> couragement devices; encourages stealing under pressure
> and mutilation — overdone — by instructors — depends
> on faculty cooperation.

Approximately three quarters of the libraries do not seat
at least 25% of the full-time-equivalent student body. These
are the same libraries having noise and conduct problems,
limited book collections and dependence on the reserve
system.

Order and quiet enforced on whatever level is commensurate with efficient and comfortable library use proved to be,
as one repondent puts it, "a loaded question." While all
agree that it is an essential goal, 17.4% find implementation
a "constant problem," due mainly to crowded conditions.
Others, with new buildings and ample facilities, emphasize
that the nature of the community college student body is
such that special consideration will always have to be provided here, in such things as adequate student lounge facilities, study halls, library locations of varying levels of
conservation and silence, adequate seating and staffing,
and library instruction and readers' advisory service.

The majority of community college library directors consider that their libraries are open for as many hours as
are needed. Some regret that they are not, but feel that it
is a question of staffing which prevents this, and a few
feel that they are open for more hours than are needed
in the sense that more hours are provided than can be
properly serviced. Certainly, the data indicate that the community college libraries are open for long hours. Too
frequently, the latest extension of library hours has been

the result of an administrative order, with "some" additional staff provided in about half the cases and none in about a quarter.

Although arrangement and servicing of materials have been well structured to facilitate their use by students and faculty of the responding community colleges, **what** is arranged and the **extent** of the services are both inadequate as judged by the ninth criterion. The effect is especially apparent in quantities of seating and staff.

Summary of the questionnaire data relevant to the ninth criterion:

there are simplified and logical arrangements of materials as well as up-to-date card catalogs with ample subject guides, analytics and cross references in most of the community college libraries, as demonstrated by such facts as 91.2% organized as one coordinated collection, 68.9% centrally and fully cataloged, and 88.3% purchasing catalog cards; to a lesser degree, evidence consists of 26.2% having a professional cataloger in charge of the catalog and technical processes, and 10.6% participating in centralized cataloging or patronizing a commercial book-processing service;

there are open stack areas in 96.1% of the community college libraries;

there are ample supplies of reserve materials to meet the special needs of 74.7% of the community colleges;

69.9% of the libraries are open to their publics for as many hours as are needed, in the opinion of their library directors;

22% of the libraries received no additional staff provision at the time library hours were last extended; 54% received "some;"

22.3% of the community college libraries are able to provide seating for at least 25% of the full-time-equivalent enrollment; of the balance, seven seat only 1-5% of the enrollment, twenty-two 6-10%, and thirteen 11-15%;

accreditation visitors' recommendations cite needed increase of physical facilities, including seating, of twenty-seven of the community colleges;

quiet is enforced on whatever level is necessary for
efficient and comfortable library use in 19.4% of the
libraries, i.e. noise and student conduct are not major
problems for only 19.4%;

only 51.4% are able to inventory annually; three (2.9%)
can spot-check only; five (4.8%) are unable to take any
regular inventory;

37.8% of the community college libraries are shared
with another institution, usually a high school; and
there is at least one staff member other than the library
director with specific audio visual responsibility in 22.3%
of the community colleges.

**X. The library is administered efficiently and effectively
within the policies of the local community college.**

Approximately two thirds of those designated as librarians
by their community colleges have fifth-year library degrees
or more, although not always from accredited programs.
This figure, of course, includes the personnel of almost
all of the "one-man" libraries and all the "one librarian"
libraries, curtailing its significance considerably.

Although approximately two thirds of the libraries have
at least two persons designated as librarians on their staffs,
there is a great lack of clerical and technical personnel,
and only about one third of the libraries are able to provide at least two staff members, one of whom is a librarian,
at all times that the library is open. Student-workers are
alone on duty in the library, including evenings, in more
than one third of the libraries, and are alone on duty at
the circulation desk in more than half of the libraries.
The waste and inefficiency of constant retraining are only
one objection to these kinds of arrangements.

The library budget is less than 5% of the college budgets
of 49.5% and not available statistically in 15.5% of the
colleges (total 65%). The picture is compounded by the fact
that during the first five years, more than 5% of the college
funds should be budgeted, and almost 20% of the questionnaire population involves community colleges founded
between 1956 and 1960. Some details of the years of founding of responding community colleges are presented in
Table 3. Library directors' comments regarding founding
include:

TABLE 3

YEARS OF FOUNDING OF RESPONDING
COMMUNITY COLLEGES

Year of founding	# of Community colleges	% of Community colleges
Prior to 1925	21	20.3%
1925-30	14	13.5
1931-35	9	8.7
1936-40	5	4.8
1941-45	1	.9
1946-50	26	25.2
1951-55	7	6.7
1956-60 i.e. less than 5 years old	20	19.4
	Total 103	100%

(There is) insufficient budgetary provision to provide reasonable standards of library service.

Money is the big problem, but as far as the community college movement is concerned the background to this need lies in the unwillingness of school officials to recognize the ways in which a college (junior college too) needs a good library. I think the worst thing that ever happened to most junior colleges is that they are run generally by local school boards.

Interpreting procedures to administration so that they can understand budget needs (is a problem). This applies also to the setting up of a junior college library. Numbers loom large. Staff is often deemed superfluous if its hours exceed the 'open hours' of the library. A new junior college should not be allowed to open without sufficient library holdings, and this means hiring a cataloging-acquisitions librarian and some clerical staff at least a year in advance to assure the 10,000-20,000 volume stock being ready to circulate on opening day. They think this is a large number . . .

Reference to faculty status of librarians was made in the questionnaire to elicit a picture of current practice insofar as community college conception of the responsibility and the personality, as it was felt that this also relates to efficient and effective library administration. Although most respondents report librarians having faculty status, statements elsewhere in their questionnaires reveal that in actual practice this is often a technicality. Librarians were found to be well qualified, due probably to state and local certification requirements. They must often have the same preparation, experience and qualifications as teaching faculty, yet they are not always treated similarly in respect to authority, status and salary. Also, their staffs are not qualified — or not paid to be. The value of state and local certification requiring the fully certified librarian to hold a fifth-year degree can be diminished by a community college with the concept of "a librarian" as library staffing.

The library directors of 58.2% of the community colleges described themselves as responsible to their college presidents, but such qualifications as "yes . . .," "yes, but," and "theoretically" were included. Throughout the questionnaires, there were frequent references to the lack of communication between library director and college president, librarians and administrators, and librarianship and educational administration. Of the six libraries seating 25% of their full-time-equivalent enrollment, and having at least 20,000 volumes and two librarians,

> three library directors report directly to their college presidents (one of these is often referred to in the literature as a community college model);

> one library director reports officially to the dean of instruction but adds that in actual practice it is to the college president; and

> two library directors report to deans of instruction, but one of these expresses dissatisfaction with the effectiveness of the arrangement and the other gives no descriptive information which reveals opinion.

A library director whose status is vague or inadequate, who lacks ultimate responsibility for book selection and expenditure of funds, who cannot expect to obtain his recommended budget or reach the chief administrator of his community college, who is not responsible for recruitment of his staff, and who is forced to rely on inadequate staffing arrangements cannot administer an efficient and effective program. Unfortunately, this is the general picture of many, although not the majority, of the participating community college libraries.

Summary of the questionnaire data relevant to the tenth criterion:

The library directors of 66.9% of the community colleges hold the fifth-year accredited library degree or more and 83.4% have faculty status;

the entire library staff consists of the respondent in 31% of the community colleges;

the library director is responsible for preparation of the budget of 73.7% of the libraries;

he/she is a member of various college committees (e.g. curriculum) in 78.6% of the community colleges;

he/she has ultimate responsibility for book selection in 61.1% of the community colleges;

79.6% of the community college reserve collections are established by faculty request (but only six, 5.8%, are established by student need in the librarian's judgment);

the library director reports to the president in 58.2% of the community colleges;

thirteen (12.6%) of the library directors are considered divisional or departmental chairmen;

56.3% are responsible for staff recruitment;

the practice of making departmental allocations restricts 29.1% of the library directors in book selection, budgeting and planning;

at least two librarians are on 66.9% of the library staffs; 30% have one librarian; the balance have "half" a librarian or none (whereas 33.9% of the community colleges have more than 2,000 students);

at least two staff members, one of whom is a professional librarian, are on duty at all times that the libraries of 33.9% of the community colleges are open to their publics;

22% of the libraries received no additional staff provision at the time library hours were last extended, 54% received "some";

student-workers are alone on duty regularly (including evenings) in 35.9% and at the circulation desk of 59.2% of the community college libraries; that is, student-workers are never alone on duty in only 58.2% nor at the circulation desk of only 27.1% of the community college libraries;

43.6% of the community college libraries employ more than five student-workers; and

the library budget is at least 5% of the current budget of only 34.9% of the community colleges.

Discussion of general community college library problems, goals and techniques reveals knowledge of the community college's place in American higher education today as well as the library's unique task in relation to it. The library directors are able to identify and fully discuss current community college library practice, "shift gears," and describe their positive and potential ideas. Respondents generally described four main ways in which their library programs aim to support the unique functions of their institutions. They aim to provide a library program comparable to that of the senior college their students are likely to attend upon graduation from the community college. They recognize the terminal students' great need for superior library service **now**, because habits of library use and thinking depend upon students' experiences at present as well as earlier. They agree that the community college library should serve as a college cultural center, provided that the first two functions have been fulfilled. And depending upon locally-identified needs and provided that the first three functions have been fulfilled, the community college library should serve as a community cultural and resource center.

Problem areas in community college library programing lie mainly in the areas of staff, physical facilities, faculty-library relations, finances, administration-library relations, collection and its organization, definition of functions and student library use. Student library use and faculty-library relations, administration-library relations and physical facilities, for example, are closely inter-related, and all areas are dependent upon financing. Where the library director is capable and provided with an adequate budget, a reasonably effective community college library program should be expected.

The respondents have ideas for solutions and innovations to make progress possible. But many community college library directors must first find some way to bring their programs **up** to a minimal basic college library one **before** they can (or should) move on to what they know is needed to further support the unique functions of the community college program. How this can be accomplished is the dilemma for which they offer suggestions. These ideas include pressure exerted from outside the community college itself, stricter academic standards supposedly resulting in a better public image of the community college and thereby a receptive taxpayer-voter, federal and other aid, improved community college administration and a closer and structured relationship between community college and library administrations. Someday of course it is hoped that improved teacher education and public school library programs will also have their effects, but they are not directly related to financing, which proves to be the crucial element in community college library support in the '60's.

Chapter IV

CASE STUDIES IN COMMUNITY
COLLEGE LIBRARY PROGRAMING

Six case studies may provide a clearer picture of current
community college library practice and its implications.
Observation of the library programs and interviews with
their directors followed completion of the questionnaire
in most cases. The data for each of these library programs
are, therefore, included in the questionnaire report. Selection
was based on such things as statistics, preliminary application of the criteria, specialized functions of the college
itself, and the library director's willingness to participate.
Although not necessarily outstanding community colleges,
they are representative of such factors as location and
environment, type of program and state of development:
a new community college in the suburbs, a technical institute-
turned community college, a junior college in a large city,
a department of a public school system, a new California
junior college district and a Southern junior college in
transition.

An attempt was made to observe several aspects of each
library program: community college environment, size, curricular emphases, physical facilities including the location
of the library present and future, and audio visual provision; library climate, physical facilities, and overt problems;
problems, limitations, unique contributions and arrangements of the library program; and the library director's
personality and expressed opinions.

Community College A: New community college in the suburbs

College A is six years old, located about eighty-five miles from New York City in a suburban environment; its enrollment consists of almost one thousand full-time students and an evening division. Its technical division offers terminal programs in business, nursery education, nursing and chemical, electrical and mechanical design technologies. All buildings on the attractive campus are new or renovated. To meet the anticipated continued growth of student body and staff, an additional classroom and laboratory building is now under construction as well as a college center which will house a theatre, music and art studios, a cafeteria, lounges and meeting rooms. Construction of a library building apparently is part of future development plans but has the lowest priority.

Responsibility for audio visual materials and services has been assigned by College A administration to a faculty member, and faculty are expected to be able to operate audio visual equipment. In actual practice, however, responsibility for audio visual materials to be used by evening classes has devolved upon the library, and the library books all films. Audio visual equipment appeared to be scattered throughout the building in classrooms which were at times unlocked.

The library was crowded with young people passing time; little work could be done at the crowded tables. The few study carrels were in great demand, but elsewhere many students were simply gathered in groups at tables. Three former living rooms on a second floor, with seating for far less than twenty five percent of the enrollment, comprised combination reading and stack rooms, and there was little shelf space left for additional acquisitions. A cataloger worked diligently at a table in the midst of one of these rooms attempting to concentrate, and at the same time supervise the room or, rather, the students in it. There was neither a general book-processing nor a cataloger's workroom. Even if there had been the latter, she would have been unable to utilize it fully because inadequate staffing required that she try to "double in brass."

Noise and stealing of books are two problems in this library. During the interview, the library director worked with the writer in the librarian's office, which was apparently a former closet with a window. The third and only other staff member, a clerk, worked in another such cubicle with no window. At the time of the writer's visit, the clerk was busy with the work resulting from the college's preparation for accreditation: surveys, questionnaires, committee activities initiated by the library director.

The "circulation desk" was at the far end of another room and staffed by a student, who was expected to carry on financial transactions with his fellow students and, if necessary, to control his peers. A student is always alone at this post, and during the evening, alone on duty in the library. At one point during the visit, a faculty member (the only one seen in the library that day) inquired as to the library's acquisition of a new book. The student referred to the card catalog. After having the book pointed out for him in the card catalog, the faculty member was unable to locate it on the shelves, but the student could not leave the desk to double-check the stacks. Nor did any charge seem to be in the circulation files. Standstill. Reader's advisory service was non-existent.

Discussion with the library director indicated that the situation was, in his opinion, initially a question of excessive administrative interference, and at present, failure to recognize the importance of the library in the college program. There are about twelve thousand books. Library budget is about 3.5% of the college budget, with some audio visual expenditures included.

There are limitations — space and budget mainly — until such time as there is a library building, but College A presents an almost classic picture of failure to recognize and provide for the prime need of staffing. Fortunately, the three staff members seem able, but at least two additional clerks are needed immediately to cover the circulation activities and other duties from early opening to late closing. The result would probably be increased circulation, decreased stealing of materials by students, decreased "borrowing" without signing for materials by faculty, increased attendance by students who would come to the library for the serious quiet fostered by the presence of an adult in the area — all resulting in far better library service in the present location.

Despite staff and space needs, the library of College A is in several ways making unique contributions to community college library service in general and its institution's program in particular. The library director has been asked to participate in State junior college library activities and does so enthusiastically. The college offerings include an associate degree program in nursing, leadership seminars and a lecture series for nurses. In support of this emphasis, a relatively large and unusual collection of related material has been assembled, including approximately twenty-five periodical titles. The library director seems to be one of few who regrets that audio visual media cannot be exploited to the fullest, and it is his goal to have audio visual facilities as part of a new library building program.

Community College B: Technical institute-turned community college

Community college B is seventeen years old, located in upstate New York in a small-city environment, although serving a county community. Its enrollment consists of about two thousand students, who are attracted by extensive technology programs. A former technical institute, the college was relocated in 1960 on a new eighty-acre site adjacent to the city and now consists of an academic building, gymnasium and student union. The library is located in the academic building, and there is a bookstore in the student union. There is talk of an "administration-library building" ultimately, but a dormitory will probably be built next.

College B's library director is serving as chairman of the State University two-year college librarians' group and when interviewed, was occupied with preparations for a workshop on the relation of the library to the junior college instructional program. She felt that, despite inadequate quarters, staffing and collection, there is some awareness on the part of the administration of these handicaps, and the main current problem is that of "devising an aggressive library program."

Some of her comments speak for themselves:
regarding the ALA Standards . . .

> The Standards serve as a guide to the junior college librarian in evaluating a given library in terms of staff, resources, services etc. — they probably receive

scant attention from administrators and are of little value in pressuring for additional staff, funds, etc.

regarding the reserve system . . .

Necessary evil — encourages dishonesty when great pressure is exerted upon a class to read the same material.

regarding things she would like to incorporate into the library program of the future . . .

Our ideal is to make the library in reality "the heart of the college". We need a strong audio visual program after careful planning has been done, adequate seating space for students and faculty, an improved system of circulation control, an organized collection of college archives, an improved catalog with complete revision of filing and recataloging where necessary, and improved service to students and faculty.

She is concerned with the average community college student's lack of study skills and library experience. Plans are being made for a testing program followed by instruction for students who do not perform satisfactorily on the test. As partial preparation for this, an experimental instruction course was offered weekly for eight weeks last year without credit.

Thought has also been given to the classification of fiction and individual biography appropriate for community college needs. A collection of separated fiction and biography was inherited from the old technical institute library, and after study of College B's updated needs and directions, reclassification was begun in 1956; all fiction and biography acquired subsequently have been classified.

The library schedules the use of audio visual equipment, administers its own collection of free audio visual materials and books and rents films. Preview facilities are limited but provision is made for listening to phonograph records. New films are purchased yearly for the technology programs. Faculty have audio visual materials and equipment picked up at the library by class members, who also operate the equipment. A problem has been retrieval of the equipment and materials after use, as the faculty tend not to return them, and it is impossible for the clerk, part of whose assignment is audio visual, to devote time to this aspect of "library service."

The library consists of one large room, adjacent stacks and three small rooms for the library director, audio visual equipment and materials, and all materials processing. Although the quarters are new to the library, i.e. not renovated, seating facilities were provided by the college in 1960 in this new building for only 4% of the enrollment. The library's most recent attempt to adjust to such planning resulted in the sacrifice of the browsing area. Library funds, exclusive of audio visual, were 3.4% of the college budget.

College B surpasses many community college libraries in its collection of almost 20,000 volumes and its staff of three professional librarians. Many of the books are, however, carryovers from the old technical institute collection. It will be necessary to redevelop the collection to support the college's move into liberal arts within the next few years, as well as to discard many passe titles in the scientific and technical areas. The situation is complicated by a backlog of books to be retrieved from departments and cataloged. These books were acquired as the result of an administration-fostered buying spree which encouraged faculty to select titles en masse at a time when there was no cataloger. A professional cataloger is now faced with both retrieval and cataloging of this uncoordinated backlog, as well as cataloging of current acquisitions including audio visual materials, the forthcoming liberal arts expansion, reclassification of fiction and biography, and an antiquated card catalog crying for revision. With the library open from 8:30 AM to 10 PM Monday through Friday and all day Saturday, it is necessary for some of her time to be spent at the circulation desk, making this total task obviously impossible.

Examples of other problems are noise and student conduct, the difficulty of obtaining approval of funds with which to bind magazines from an "anti-binding" college administration, involvement of indifferent evening-division faculty (and thereby, students), and the necessity of employing too many students.

One crowded room and the presence of students at the desk in that room inevitably make for noise and distraction in the library. Many College B students are adolescents with interests in quick and easy vocational preparation. There is a constant turnover of student employees who are unable or unwilling to do the meticulous and sometimes dirty work of library maintenance, especially when there is other employment available. Even were it possible to make this kind of work competitive and always appealing, the constant and inadequate retraining would persist, and on any campus, the most conscientious and intelligent student is not capable of supervising and serving a library crowded with his peers.

Community College C: Junior college in a large city

College C is six years old, located in a large Midwestern city. One of the newer branches of the city junior college operating as part of the public school system, it functions in many ways as a community college in a semi-residential and industrial neighborhood some distance from the center of the city. Its enrollment is about two thousand five hundred, approximately half of whom are fulltime students. Probably one third of the total enrollment plan to transfer to the state university. Others are taking late afternoon and evening classes with no special plan: housewives taking child psychology, graduate students from other institutions taking Russian, future tourists taking Spanish, secretaries brushing up stenography, others enrolled in such terminal programs as food service and electronic and chemical technologies.

In line with the board of education pattern, College C was imposed upon one of the already existing high schools serving this part of the city, sharing almost the entire plant in late afternoon and evening and having some of its own facilities assigned for day and evening use, including a former study hall for a college library. The high school library facilities, staff and collection are entirely separate from, and larger than, those of the college. Community College C has less than 6,000 volumes in its collection. It is difficult to determine the amount or percent budgeted for maintenance of the college library program, and it is always unpredictable. Some funds come through the board of education and others from the individual college budget. Support from the board is graduated and somewhat automatic, always delayed; "local" funds involve competition

with instructional departments and administrative needs.
A college pattern is the assignment of complete responsibility
for audio visual materials, equipment, maintenance and
service to the library.

The college has gradually expanded its electronics technology program with government assistance until it now
occupies one wing of the plant, while provision for the
library remains static. The library director has succeeded
in obtaining use of an adjacent room for workspace and in
convincing departmental chairmen of the library's needs,
so that they are willing to approve some college funds for
library use. Several major private libraries located in the
same city have had to curtail use by Community College
C's students, indicating in communication with English
and social science departments that students lacked sufficient
"subject matter background and library experience" to
utilize the libraries without imposing a burden on both staffs
and resources which would exclude the rights of others
whose research needs were greater. Community College C's
library director has worked out a compromise by means of
which qualified students receive a letter of introduction from
her validating their need.

The library is open weekdays from 8 AM to 10 PM,
and is staffed by two full-time librarians and two civil service clerks. Since it is responsible for all of its own processing and cataloging of materials as well as the audio visual
program, it is clear that College C's greatest need is staff.
Cumbersome book ordering procedures and civil service
clerical arrangements result from being under the board
of education and part of the city school system.

College C's library program is making contributions
in three areas which reflect the institution's unique functions.
Students who plan to transfer to the state university or
other senior college are largely recent graduates of the
city's high schools, which provide little or no library experience. While at College C, their library experience should
in a sense be a "catch-up" one. The library program attacks
this problem with required orientation, close work with the
college counselor, sponsorship of a library-audio visual
club, special training for student assistants, and acquisition
of library-related audio visual materials.

College C has neither a student lounge nor lockers — no

central home base for its day students, who often arrive from work; the library seats far less than twenty-five percent of the enrollment (seven percent) in one room. Nevertheless, quiet is literally enforced at a level so that those students who wish to study and do research may do so; this requires an almost impossible and unpopular effort involving the constant attempt to obtain student, faculty and library staff cooperation, and a distribution of library staff which spreads its resources too thin. There is little opportunity for the two librarians to confer, none for staff meetings.

Even so, another contribution to its community college program has been made; the cooperation, behind the scenes, of the high school and college librarians has improved relations between the host high school and the college.

Community College D: Department of the public school system

Community College D has been in operation continuously since 1930 as a department of the public school system, and is so described in the catalog. It is located in a Midwestern county seat of 4,000 population drawing from a county population of 15,000 within a twenty-five mile radius. The junior college, as it is more often called, has planned its courses to articulate with upper division work of state institutions.

The college is located in the high school building, and students may utilize the school bus at cost. There are one hundred two students in Community College D and twenty-one faculty members including administrative and part-time personnel. Admission is based on graduation from an approved high school, recommendation by that school, distribution of preparatory courses, and College Entrance Examination scores. The junior college dean is designated as counselor, and the purpose of the guidance program is to help the student to "adjust himself to the life and work of the college, to obtain the education best adapted to his needs and abilities, and to adjust himself to personal, social, religious and vocational problems." It is not clear just how this is achieved. An elective Orientation Course purports to provide "improvement of study skills" for students "with poor reading and study habits" — the one reference to the library program in the college catalog appears in this context.

Community College D seems to illustrate the case of the public junior college which assumes the designation of community college but does not fully develop those aspects of higher education unique and essential to this kind of program. Tuition is "low cost", $140. per year for residents, but one wonders whether **any** tuition plus living costs can be supported by young people living in the agricultural, rural, non-industrialized community.

Curricula include agriculture, elementary or secondary education, engineering, home economics, science, pre-veterinary-medicine and nursing — all geared to fit into four-year programs. Accounting, secretarial science and business management, however, may be pursued as terminal programs. An adult-education ten-week program provided during the winter months costs from $3. to $5. per session. Evening college credit courses are given only when there is a large enrollment.

The librarian of Community College D, like most of her colleagues, has a master's degree, is a part-time staff member, and has adapted herself to her assignment. A high school teacher for forty years, she received this assignment about ten years ago and since then has been responsible for the combination high school-junior college library. She feels that, as a former teacher, her standards of student conduct and performance are stricter than they would be otherwise. Not only is Community College D's "librarian" doubling-in-brass as librarian of two distinct institutions with dissimilar student bodies, levels of work and interests, but she is their entire staff and compensated on a part-time basis for her junior college work. She describes Community College D's library's greatest need to be a librarian, for in reality it has neither librarian nor library. The high school library, actually a library-study hall, is crowded with its two hundred fourteen students and one hundred two junior college students. A consultant from the state teachers college was employed in the early 1950's, but only some of her recommendations were implemented . . . weeding, for example. In the last accrediting visit, a recommendation that a better line of demarcation between college and high school student-areas be made in the library resulted in a shelving divider separating the high school study hall desks and the college library tables. Books are on open shelves with one common catalog. High school students may use the tables for reference with large volumes, but junior college students have priority at the tables.

Community College D's audio visual program is not a library responsibility. Audio visual materials are handled by one faculty member in charge of the area for both the high school and the junior college.

Faculty do not regularly make recommendations for the library collection and program, and the materials which are on hand for professional use are utilized only occasionally. The library does not subscribe to THE JUNIOR COLLEGE JOURNAL because the college receives a copy as part of its membership in the American Association of Junior Colleges — an obviously necessary economy.

Library orientation attendance is offered at the beginning of the term, but not required. Plans are being made to purchase a film for this purpose. The science and history departments maintain informal book collections, but their very informality made it difficult for the librarian to indicate the nature or extent of their content. The library is of course unable to provide all materials needed in the ordinary course of the students' work. It is necessary for even the average student to depend on other libraries and sources at least occasionally. But the only other library is the 16,000-volume public library. Most book loans are for reserve books over short periods. The librarian states that, "We have many books which would be used to better advantage if faculty acquainted themselves with them." In her opinion, the library collection does provide sufficient coverage to stimulate the best students and to serve the faculty, but what they do have could be used more fully.

The junior college library of course does not have twenty thousand volumes nor does it even entertain this figure as a working-goal. In fact, it is difficult to determine the number of its holdings, although it can be said that there are five thousand volumes in the high school library. Acquisition of basic tools and indexes is out of the question. Out of print books must be kept under lock. The library budget is currently 3.5% of the junior college budget. The catalog description of "the full cooperation of the local

Carnegie public library, which provides many of the finest
current publications as well as excellent reference materials"
reminds one of the headlines in professional and popular
literature . . . NO PLACE TO READ: BOOK SHORTAGE
IN SCHOOLS BLAMED FOR LIBRARIES' TRAFFIC
JAMS . . . HELP NEEDED . . . CRISIS IN THE PUB-
LIC LIBRARIES . . . LIBRARIES INADEQUATE.[38]
Community College D's librarian is responsible and
reports to the college dean. She does not recommend a
library budget — "budget minima are set by the state."
The students often are alone in the library, since it is open
from 8 A.M. to 5 P.M. and two evenings. It is interesting to
to note that withal, Community College D's librarian's summary of problem areas is consistent with those of community college library directors all over the country: need for
better use of existing materials, personnel, and space. It is
probable that concurrently maintaining a library-study hall
for two hundred fourteen high school adolescents and a library collection for one hundred two junior college young
adults, in the same room, single-handedly, is her unique
contribution to the program of Community College D!

Community College E: New California junior college district

The inspiring history of Community College E culminated
in the opening of a new $11,500,000 campus in 1961.
Thirty-nine buildings have been coordinated on a large,
convenient and attractive campus planned for four-thousand
day students and an equal number of evening students.
As it happens, Community College E's title does not include
this term, but follows the California "junior college" pattern.
It aims to serve a new junior college district encompassing
one hundred five square miles, or two high school and one
unified school districts, or a large segment of one county.
By 1963, enrollment had reached three thousand two
hundred.

Community College E grants the AA degree; admission
is open to graduates, with C average, of accredited high
schools, and others over nineteen years of age are admittable
on probation. A great variety of terminal programs is
offered in the college's tuition-free program. These are
collectively called "technical education and professional
assistants programs" and include computer programming,

procurement and supply, and x-ray technician, to mention a few of the more unusual. Despite an impressive terminal program, the college catalog and student handbook play up aspects of the curriculum and program which would interest the prospective transfer student. A "Halls of Ivy"-atmosphere prevails, with descriptions of such "traditions" as college colors, mascot, festival, queen and rival football games. A speakers' bureau operated free of charge by the college is one example of the many community services developed by Community College E.

The library program occupies one full page (of twenty-three) in the student handbook, and the library building is the largest single construction on campus. It is the highest building, a focal point, and located at the center of the group of academic buildings. In addition to a large reading room there is a reference room, reading patio, listening room, and group study, typing, recording and preview-listening rooms. Students have direct access to the main collection. A rapid expansion of the book collection has increased it to about 20,000 volumes; there is space for further expansion to 76,000. Tapes, phonorecords, pamphlets, government documents, vocational materials, periodicals and reserve materials are also on hand. The typing room provides coin-operated machines and tables for students bringing their own portables as well as a service table with ink, paper-cutter, punch, stapler and so forth. Use of the Group Study Room and the Preview-Listening Rooms is scheduled at the Loan Desk. A single controlled exit with inspection of materials is part of the floor-plan. The library is open from 8 A.M. until 10 P.M. on school days, Friday until 4:30 and Sunday from 1 to 5 P.M.

The new junior college district served by Community College E was established in 1957, its president reported for work the following year, and its library director was recruited five months later — the same month classes began in a temporary location. The library director is in the administrative group and works with administrative committees, divisional chairmen and on the curriculum committee. A recommendation concerning the library program made as a result of the last accrediting visit urged faculty to be more active in requesting books. Presumably to imple-

ment this, the accrediting team also suggested departmental
book budget allocations, despite the fact that faculty had
always been notified of new publications and urged to
make requests.

The library director is chairman of a library committee
which consists of one representative from each division
elected by the divisional faculty, one from the counseling
staff, and all of the professional library services staff. "It
is advisory on policy, serves as a liaison with faculty and
is most effective in providing communication with faculty."
A minimum of four hours weekly is spent by the library
director in meetings of college groups and committees,
such as the curriculum committee. She is also active in
the several public library organizations in the area.

A library handbook is sold in the students' store and
used in connection with an elective orientation course. Library orientation, however, is required of all new full-time
students early in the term. Two lecture sections (tape-slide
presentations), a worksheet to be answered in the library
and a quiz on the material are given. Since the course
covers only rules, procedures, arrangement of books and
use of the catalog and READERS' GUIDE, it is inadequate
in the opinion of the library director. "But it is all that
five librarians can do with fifteen hundred freshman in
the time allotted." Having examined the orientation films
on the market and concluded that their tape-slide presentation is better for their situation, the library staff is considering converting these into 16mm films.

There is little response to the constant recommendations
made to English teachers to have librarians speak to classes
on specific materials related to term papers. A library
instruction course is offered, but it is an elective. Taught
by the librarians, it meets once a week and provides one
credit. Its aim is to familiarize students with library resources
and reference books, but it is designed for transfer students.
Regarding the library technology curriculum, the library
director comments that, "A few California junior colleges
offer this curriculum with very small enrollment. Salaries
for library clerks are no higher than for general clerks,
so students do not enroll in the more difficult program."

The library program does not include a library-audio
visual club because it is "considered too high-schoolish."

Book talks — usually panel discussions by instructors — are sponsored by the library several times a year, but "We have such a full club, lecture and so forth program that **any** event is difficult to schedule!"

The average student borrows more of his books from the general collection of Community College E's library than from the reserve collection. The librarians select about one third of the titles purchased on the basis of scholarly reviews and subject bibliographies. In the judgment of the library director, the collection provides sufficient coverage to stimulate the best students and to serve the faculty. "The faculty say our collection is good and compare it favorably with new books in other college libraries." Since the college is only four and a half years old, its library collection is weak in older material and back issues of serials. All of the standard indexes are subscribed to. The success in book selection and in keeping the collection up-to-date are, according to Community College E's library director's refreshing and simple comment, the result of "an adequate book budget, professional librarians, and an alert faculty!"

Two hundred fifty periodicals are regularly received, ten in foreign languages, and one hundred eighty are bound. Eleven newspapers are received. The library program provides the college audio visual materials but not services. Fifty four films were purchased in one year and eight hundred fifty eight were borrowed or rented. The audio visual coordinator, although a participant in the library program, has a background in radio and television rather than in librarianship. An audio visual clerk and a technician, as well as student assistants, are employed in the audio visual program.

The library director considers the reserve system a necessary evil, for "what library can supply one copy of a required supplementary reading for five hundred students the night before a test?" Sunday hours were added this year upon the library director's recommendation after a student survey to indicate which four weekend hours would be most convenient. "Of course, some students would come in at any hour the library was open." At the time this recommendation was implemented, the college administration provided an additional professional librarian for the added time as well as student help.

Seating in this new library building was provided for 16% of the anticipated enrollment. Even so, it is not possible to enforce quiet on a level necessary for efficient and comfortable library use. "We need more staff to enforce it. One room seating one hundred eighty-four has no supervisory desk." And now the reading patio will soon have to be enclosed to provide additional space.

The library director reports formally to the dean of instruction, informally to the college president. She is responsible for preparation of the library budget and recruitment of the library staff. She has the ultimate responsibility for book selection and for expenditure of book funds. There are no departmental library budget allocations.

The professional library staff consists of the director of library services, the coordinator of audio visual services, three and a half other librarians, a half-time circulation clerk, and four other clerks one of whom is the audio visual clerk. A graphic artist is employed on an hourly basis. All of the library staff, including some of the clerks, have Master's degrees. The library director is the only librarian whose professional training was not in an ALA-accredited program. Eleven student assistants are employed part-time in the library-audio visual program. There are at least two staff members, one of whom is a professional librarian, on duty at all times that the library is open to its public. Student workers are never alone on duty in the library nor at the circulation desk. The annual library maintenance budget of Community College E is 5.9% of the institutional budget, but this includes audio visual materials.

In California, while junior college librarians theoretically have faculty status, they are paid from a different budget category than classroom teachers. The salaries for classroom teachers must be at least 50% of the general education budget, so, even in wealthy districts, administrators may find it difficult to get librarians, counselors, clerks, books and so forth from the remaining 50%. It is generally claimed in California that junior college counseling services and laboratories are equal or superior to those of state colleges. This cannot be said of the libraries.

The library director was asked to describe what she sees as the unique needs and functions of the community college movement.

In some ways, a community college covers a broader range of students and more diverse subject matter than a university. By law, California junior colleges must admit all high school graduates and those over eighteen years who may profit from their program. They try to be all things to all people — lower division university transfer; vocational and technical institutes; general education institutions (non-transfer).

Regarding problems areas,

The chief problem is always adequate financial support, as evidenced in many ways: lack of facilities, lack of personnel, lack of budget for purchases, lack of top instructors skilled in using library materials and interested in helping their students to do likewise.

She strongly favors the ALA junior college standards, "taking into account that the local situation requires interpretation, as stated in the Standards." She would like to incorporate into Community College E's library program all-carrel seating, a microfilm collection for periodicals earlier than 1960, duplicate subscriptions of all periodicals, and provision of study-hall space out of the library for students who are not using library materials.

Community College F: Southern junior college in transition

Community College F serves a Southern, urban junior college district. It sometimes refers to itself as a community college. It is proud of its faculty, many of whom hold a master's degree. Although established in 1934, two units of a new plant were occupied in 1951. The main building housed classrooms, laboratories, library and offices; the second unit was the gymnasium. In 1958, a "liberal arts" building containing offices, student lounge, faculty lounge, cafeteria and bookstore was occupied. Enrollment is now about twelve hundred full-time students. Established under junior college legislation enacted by the state, Community College F is supported chiefly by local taxation augmented by fees and tuition ($100 per year).

A new air-conditioned library building seating seven hundred students and providing space for 75,000 volumes has recently been occupied. A collection of 28,000 volumes and 236 periodicals has been built up, possibly at the expense of other aspects of the library program. The library aims to provide service for college students and residents of the district, all of whom make a $10 refundable library deposit. There is "complete cooperation" between the nearest public library and the community college library, for instance in avoiding duplication of technical periodicals and in inter-library loan service. High school students doing "research" in the college library must present a form from the high school librarian showing that the school cannot supply the need. A public university thirty miles away allows Community College F students library use upon presentation of the same type of letter. In addition, there is a county library for the use of all. Community College F's library director considers all of these arrangements to be excellent.

Both the Associate of Arts and Applied Arts diplomas are granted. Terminal programs in such fields as air-conditioning, refrigeration, automotive mechanics, welding, pipe-fitting and electricity are referred to as "nonacademic courses." "Adult courses" at the end of the day are also offered.

The catalog admonishes the student that final responsibility for choice of the proper courses must rest with him, although faculty advisers "will gladly assist a student in selecting the courses that will assure him full standing in a senior institution." Two Bible courses are included in the course offerings. Each student is assigned to a faculty member who serves as his counselor during the year. There is a director of testing and counseling. No smoking is permitted. A large number of activities includes a student NEA chapter, Baptist student union, Wesley Foundation, Reb-Belles and the Confederate Ball. Approximately the same amount of space allotted to parking regulations is provided for the library program in the student handbook. A required freshman orientation course allocates about three meetings of its seventeen-week activities to "Knowing your library."

The library is open from 8 A.M. to 9:30 P.M. Monday through Thursday and from 8 A.M. to 4:30 P.M. on Friday. There is space for students who wish to bring their typewriters and two conference rooms are available for group study. Such facilities, a student lounge, and library seating for 25% of the student body make possible a minimum of disturbance and necessary control in the library. There are two "librarians"; one has had no library training and the other is a diplomate of an unaccredited program. One of the three clerks is a diplomate of Community College F. Eight regularly-scheduled student assistants are required to do part-time clerical work, while four work at the checking door. It is necessary to leave student assistants alone at the circulation desk.

The library director voiced a preference "to have full-time staff members do some things now done by students. Re-training problems are heavy and efficiency is not up to par." Innovations are open shelves and a door checkout system, which, however, is maintained by students. In the last accrediting visit, the new library building and an enlarged staff were recommended. The library director supports the ALA junior college standards but feels that they are "barely high enough — too many loop-holes for poorly operated libraries or perhaps I should say, for non-library minded administrators to fail to do what needs to be done budget-wise for their libraries." Four faculty members and the librarian are appointed by the academic dean to constitute a library committee. Its effectiveness "depends on the members — some years it is very poor and at other times it serves well to keep faculty members informed of library needs and purposes and to interpret procedures to those concerned."

Community College F maintains an audio visual department which is not part of the library program although the library, of course, includes phonograph records in its collection. Although the librarian is restricted to one third of the book funds and the balance is allocated to departments, she reports that faculty weed the collection and do order for it, and do not "overdo" reserve collections. The library maintenance budget has been allocated 5% of the college budget. With the new library building and a shortage of library staff, it would seem that most of these maintenance funds are being used to build up the book collection quantitatively. Community College F's librarian ranks problem areas in the order of staff, budget, faculty-library relationships, and administration-library relationships. She states that,

The junior college library is in the unique position of carrying more responsibility in the development of cultural standards than is any other library, for its aims are the same as those of the institution. Culture and education are concerned with the intellectual side of civilization and involving the spiritual, mental and mechanical improvement. This then is the unique need and function of the junior college library: to assist in the development of discrimination and understanding, to assist in the growth and refinement of education and training, instead of the usual 'reading for recreation, education, etc.'.

Because young people are anxious to get away from home and into the popular universities, the community college does not get the cross section of the better students, often only those who need to take advantage of the financial saving. I feel that more worthwhile social and intellectually stimulating activities on college level might help in this area. The acceptance of the college's contribution — realization is perhaps a better word — by the community is vital to its growth.

The library suffers most of all because the public is unaware or uninformed about its contribution to the community and to the lives of the students. Open-house, exhibits open to the public, lectures, book reviews open to public **might** help **if** they were permitted or if there were money available. Staff to maintain a good library is often a major problem. It is hard to sell administrators the idea of adding staff members to give more or better service; they haven't had to add more teachers, so why can't the library take care of the same enrollment as last year . . .

Chapter V

THE FUTURE OF THE
COMMUNITY COLLEGE LIBRARY PROGRAM

A realistic evaluation of current community college library practice discloses as much recognition of the unique functions of the institution as exists elsewhere in the community college itself. It is particularly evident in the attempts made to provide for the unique community college student himself: for example, seating sufficient to provide for large numbers of unbased day students on undeveloped campuses, library instruction to supplement deficient backgrounds, professional readers' advisory service to help compensate for mediocre teaching and mass textual reading assignments. Collections which are broad as well as deep are advocated by community college library directors, who recognize that the community college library program has the responsibility to provide more than a collegiate collection, that the community college student is not the traditional college student, and that the community college library is one place in the program where part of his uniqueness can be enhanced or compensated for, as the case may be.

Many community college libraries have incorporated these goals and plans into their programs. Yet in actual practice, these needs are not consistently met; these plans are not carried out; these goals are not fulfilled. In fact, minimal basic collegiate library service is not generally provided. In the case of the new community college, administration often does not recruit a capable library director at least a year before first classes not only because there is a shortage, but also because the need is not recognized and assigned a priority in recruitment and planning. It follows

that the library program is not planned nor is the basic
collection ready for first classes. Furthermore the library
is often allocated space in a building designated and designed for some other purpose.

Many library directors reported that the majority of community college instructors make little or no effort, aside
from requesting books to be placed on reserve, to integrate
library use and course work, and that special efforts by the
faculty to encourage general reading are negligible. (However, "capable, interested and effective" faculties were reported in six cases.) The comments given below from the
questionnaire report are illuminating:

> Faculty (members), promoted to a junior college after
> years of high school teaching, sometimes bring their
> high school teaching ways with them. Their assignments
> do not have the breadth and scope that require much
> library research and delving into books. The student
> does not become adept in library research.

> Many instructors lack the special training and experience
> needed in the community college.

> (A problem) is the instructor who gives required read-
> ings and informs the library after the class. It's the
> same story everywhere, I know, but there are more
> part-time faculty in the community college.

> The community college is just more high school, so the
> college library is more high school library.

> The 'psychologist' displays and distributes so-called
> vocational guidance materials although he apparently
> cannot distinguish between commercial mailings and
> factual presentation, between advertisements and relevant
> information. The students are confused by what they
> read as well as by the impression they receive thusly
> that all vocational material is free for the taking!

> Full-time faculty will more likely have their first loyalty
> to the community college.

The qualifications of the community college teacher are
directly related to the success of the community college
library program. He may be a former high school teacher
who regards this as a step up from the classroom, or he

may yet be a high school teacher working "over time" in his own system or community. His pattern of teaching, and his experience and outlook inevitably differ from those needed by the community college teacher. Or, he may be the part-time teacher from business or industry whose prime interest or ability is in the office, factory, or laboratory. There is also the transient teacher whose personal goal is "advancement" to a senior college, and whose concern for the community college library's blatent inadequacies in terms of both current practice and goals is non-existent. Large classes, inexperience, student aptitude and attitude may lead teachers to utilize lecture-type teaching methods exclusively, with library use, if any, consisting of misuse of the reserve system with required mass reading assignments from textual materials. This may result in stealing and destruction of reserve materials by students, as well as lack of use of other materials and warped attitudes toward all libraries.

The community college with an active, library-oriented faculty and a student body challenged by high standards and inspired teaching requires a library program providing a variety of subject matter on reading and interest levels to encompass the students' varied abilities and academic programs. Such a library program will also provide for the other designated functions which, although not always fulfilled in the classroom, are assumed by the community college.

The nature of the public library program, the population boom and the educational expansion of the college-age group make it essential that the community college provide all library materials needed by its students and faculty. They cannot depend on other community outlets nor can they be excused from library use by default. In fact, the true community college would be able to contribute to the community library program, and it is interesting and propitious to note that a few community college libraries are able to serve their communities as academic reference libraries.

Of the one hundred three responding community colleges, only six have at least 20,000 volume collections, seating for 25% of the full-time-equivalent enrollment, and a staff of at least two professional librarians. Of these six above-average programs, only three have budgets which are at least 5% of the college budget, and they are barely 5%. There are three general conclusions from comparison of current community college library practice with the criteria established. The community college library needs an overall general improvement quantitatively and qualitatively to provide minimal basic library service. When discussing problems and limitations upon effectiveness and success of their programs, community college library directors cite the areas of quantity of collections, physical facilities (especially seating), and adequate staffing. Of the community college libraries represented, 63.1% have less than 20,000 volumes; 74.7% lack seating for at least 25% of their students; and, in 31% of them, the respondent comprises the entire library staff.

Although there are varied general as well as specialized ways in which the library program can best serve the unique needs and functions of the community college program, the library is now most often unable to serve its institution effectively because it lacks financial support. The library directors' statements include reminders that such conditions add up to the problem of budgetary provision. The suggestion that they produce ingenious and unique techniques of library service to the community college is futile, for all of their efforts are spent on maintenance of a day-to-day program with the means currently provided them.

There is evidence that current practice is based on the library director's knowledge of techniques of professional library service and the unique functions of the community college. Where library programs do not demonstrate this vividly, the main reason is lack of funds. While library staffs as a whole are generally inadequate in numbers and in training and experience, the library directors for the most part are well-trained and enlightened, with resourceful approaches and techniques for sustaining their libraries under depressing conditions. There is need to assist them in their efforts to receive an adequate budget.

A Plan for Action

The community college student is as unique as his institution. He is not always the traditional collegiate young

person nor has he always had the traditional college preparation or background, including "library background."
His secondary school may have had no library program.
Or he may be older and have forgotten any library skills
he may have had.

Since an individual of any age is rarely willing or able
to take the initiative in mastering the techniques of library
usage needed for minimal college work and an adequate
previous library experience is not in the background of
many community college students, library orientation takes
on increased importance. Collegiate library usage implies,
in addition to control of library resources, a close relationship to freedom of thought, creativity, independent thinking
and personal development, and it is the handmaiden of
inspired teaching. The ability, need and desire to use a
library and to be part of an active library program are
especially important to the community college student today.
Furthermore, the library program is a particularly important supportive element in the community college program because of the need for materials and services for the
varied community college students' interests and abilities
as indicated in the unique terminal programs, especially
technologies; transfer student programs; individual courses,
workshops, conferences, experiences; and vocational, educa-
cational and personal guidance.

The community college must provide for all of its students'
library needs. Aside from the inequities involved in imposing
numbers of community college students upon other libraries
in the community, it is highly improbable that the students
will or can make the effort. Specialized libraries are not
equipped to provide for masses of community college students inexperienced in library usage or for their types of
needs. The public library program by definition is generally
not an academic one; moreover, the great increase in teen-
age population, revision in teaching methods, and inadequate public school library programs have already created
a burden on public libraries which the community college
influx only intensifies. If the resources of other community
libraries are misused in this way, their value as occasional
inter-library loan participants decreases and the rare and
specialized books which should be shared among cooperative libraries cease to be available.

It follows that special emphases in community college library programing are needed in instruction, collection, seating and other facilities and staffing. Specifically, this means instruction beyond orientation to enable students to use library resources, to step beyond the textbook, to supplement classroom methods, to make their use of a library more than a high school study hall experience. It means quantities of well selected books to provide library materials on several levels for many interests and abilities — academic, personal, vocational. It means seating for exceptionally large numbers of non (or low) — paying, non-resident, often disoriented and unbased students with high school library habits at best. And it means staffing which will provide the personnel to make such a program possible: a library administrator, a cataloger, a readers' adviser, someone with audio visual responsibility, clerks, part-time student employees who must not be depended upon to perform essential clerical work.

These add up to the need for a general drastic improvement of current community college library practice in order to bring it up to a minimal basic college library standard. Then and only then can a unique community college library program be built up. Funds are needed as well as an attitude change and recognition of these factors by all community college personnel.

If the community college library program is to assist in the fulfillment of the institution's unique functions, if positive life-time reading and thinking habits are to be formed, if indeed there is justification for a community college library, the community college administrator must act. The support of the college administrator is essential for implementation of the recommendations for the improved library program.

The community college administrator should ascertain whether the interests of the library program are best served. With the library director, he should study the library's organization, staffing, problems and goals to determine how well they fulfill instructional and other functions. Wise decisions in the areas of each of the following recommendations will be based on such an attitude of concern.

Community college administrators and planners should make every effort to obtain a capable library director at the earliest possible moment in college development. Data submitted by the library directors of recently established community colleges indicate that many of the problems would have been eliminated had a capable library director been employed along with the first faculty and at least a year before first classes.

A minimum of 5% of the community college budget should be devoted to the library maintenance program exclusive of audio visual after the first five years of the college. In new community colleges, basic library collection and equipment should be part of initial financial outlay, planned and developed before first classes. Where community colleges are going into new buildings, the library director should be able to work with the architect. Many inadequate and unsuccessful community college library programs have been the result of the assumption that basic book stock could be acquired over a period of years, even though the annual budget available for the community college library is often inadequate for current maintenance. Funds should be provided for the minimal library program described by the ALA Standards. Data indicate that special emphases are at present needed in the areas of staffing, physical facilities and collection.

The need for exceptionally well qualified community college faculty should be recognized as directly related to the success of the library program. Students who are not challenged and who are permitted to do minimal, routine work will not become independent resourceful library users nor for that matter, successful college students and citizens. Provision of teachers who will educate rather than train is essential if appropriate attitudes, skills and habits are to be developed on all three of these levels. Community junior college specialists are as needed as subject specialists.

Community college libraries should be entirely independent of the libraries of other institutions. Neither the community college library nor the library with which it is combined is able to provide an adequate library program when administered in combination. The abilities and reading interests of high school and junior college students especially are too far apart to be compatible. In the establishment of new community colleges, the need for a separate and independent community college district should be recognized. In older

community colleges, attachments and relationships to other
governing bodies, districts, etc. should be minimized and
elimination fostered if possible. Examples of problems resulting for the community college library are student attitude that the community college is "more high school",
time-consuming and unwieldy purchasing and ordering
arrangements, and antiquated civil service staffing which
makes it impossible to obtain or retain satisfactory clerical
personnel.

The library director should have faculty status equivalent
to that of departmental chairman. The data indicate that,
while this factor is important in all collegiate library leadership work, clarification is especially needed for the community college library director who so often must build up
a new library program as well as carry on considerable
leadership work. The library director should be responsible
for his budget, materials and staff selection, and program.
He should not be restricted by departmental allocations.
The data indicate that limitations imposed by administration upon library director's authority in these areas are
important deterrents to his effectiveness.

The local organization and ways of working should be
such that the library director has communication with the
community college president and the academic dean. Whether
this means that he would report directly to the president or
to the academic dean will vary with factors in the local
situation. There is no one best method of assuring the
sympathetic and ready interest on the part of the college
administration which is sought here. In any event, no
community college president can hope to have his institution function and grow without giving adequate support
to this important institutional component. Communication
between the community college library director and faculty
should be facilitated by placing the library director on such
college committees as the curriculum committee. Recognition
that an administration-appointed faculty library committee
does not achieve the necessary relationship will foster the
library director's invitation to qualified, interested faculty
to form a library committee.

The following recommendations are directed to the community college library director. They should be thought of

as existing in a framework of the recommendations directed to the college administrator.

There should be support for and implementation of the ALA Standards, especially in the areas of staffing, collection and seating. The library director should utilize the Standards to guide in providing for the unique functions of his individual institution. This will usually necessitate emphasis on student use and faculty integration of library resources.

Special provision to meet the unique needs of the community college student through library instruction and staffing is recommended. As indicated by the library directors, efforts by instructors to integrate library use and coursework, aside from reserves, are unimpressive, and their efforts to encourage general reading are negligible. Students who plan to transfer to senior colleges usually do not have community college library facilities nor experiences comparable to those of the first two years of the senior colleges, and many new community college students do not already possess library skills or attitudes. Provision for required adequate library instruction, rather than the traditional orientation to new facilities (which assumes general knowledge of library techniques and resources) is therefore essential. A library instruction course should be required of all new full-time community college students and library orientation provided for others. Recognition of the unusual need to foster lifetime reading habits on the part of a student body with little inclination or ability to utilize library resources will aid in obtaining staff to implement this recommendation. There should be continuous, professional readers' advisory service to provide for the special needs of community college students and faculty. The readers' adviser should be thought of in a new and broad sense comparable to the community college's expansion of the higher education provision. He should provide an instructional program ranging from orientation for students needing only a refresher to a course for new full-time students, lectures and laboratory work with specific classes at teachers' requests, and a testing program, possibly in cooperation with the college freshman orientation program. He should encourage regular faculty conferences and workshops for all kinds of community college personnel and individual student guidance in the library context. He should be responsible for preparation and distribution of library bulletins and other materials and publications, effective displays, and leadership of library and audio visual-sponsored programs, as well as student and faculty library handbooks. Ultimately, he should work with community libraries to develop cooperative arrangements. And above all, the readers' adviser provides the presence of a library faculty member in the midst of the library itself, ready to consult effectively but unobtrusively with students about problems of reference, bibliography and the use of the card catalog.

At least two staff members, one of whom is a librarian, should be on duty whenever the library is open to its public. There should be at least two librarians on the staff of every community college library. Clerical personnel, rather than students, should be assigned to circulation desk duty. Student employees should be utilized for shelving, shelf-reading, deliveries, etc. and in connection with a library technology curriculum. Clerks, technicians and subprofessionals should be employed in a one-to-one ratio to librarians. The data in this study show a close relationship between the creation of new staff positions in the community college library and public judgment of what is obviously essential to good library service. Library directors with adequate provision for staffing are able to redistribute staff assignments and responsibilities as the first steps towards improved community college library programing. Implementation of this recommendation is also, therefore, in the community college administrator's area.

Community college library planning should include the provision of a basic collection of at least 20,000 titles, fully cataloged and processed, ready for classes. The community college library program should be developed to provide for all of its students' and most of its faculty's library needs. There should be active participation in professional library and inter-library activities, primarily as a loaner, borrowing mainly for the faculty. The data point to the community college library imposing on the community and other libraries. Instead it should be able to contribute to community library service in education reference and leadership.

The reserve system as presently conceived should be deemphasized and replaced with open reserves, course shelves and almost no closed reserves. Open reserves are usually fairly large collections of materials which have been segregated from the general collection and limited in loan period, but accessible for browsing. Closed reserves differ in that they must be "called for" at a circulation desk and are often available for an hour's room use or overnight at the end of the day. They tend to be text-book-type materials, required mass readings designated by faculty. Course shelves are browsing collections pertaining to one course or to one group's interest, similar to open reserves. Evidence that the present closed reserve system is "over-done," conducive to rigid and shallow thinking as well as limited library programing is overwhelming. It appears not just in the replies to questions bearing directly on reserve system, but throughout the questionnaires and in the library directors' comments on such things as faculty utilization of library resources, student use of the general collection and results of inadequate book collections.

A new community college library should be planned to include a library classroom, open stacks to accommodate a collection of at least 30,000 volumes and other ample storage, workroom, cataloging and office facilities, study carrels, student conference and typing rooms, browsing area, seating for at least 25% of the anticipated full-time-equivalent enrollment and controlled, single exit flow of traffic.

Several ideas and techniques were mentioned by library directors as possible supportive means to better community college library programing. They felt that it is the responsibility of their group to encourage development of certain products as well as to be willing to experiment with the output. The support of the profession should be given to the movement to produce an up-to-date basic bibliography for community college library collection planning, to perfecting commercial and centralized processing, to all types of relevant publications, to a 10,000-cataloged-titles package and to production of a film suitable for community college library instruction.

The audio visual program should be housed in the library building and coordinated with the library program. There

should be at least one member of the community college
staff who is an audio visual specialist and able to devote
full-time to the audio visual program. A local audio visual
presentation should be prepared for use in library instruction, preferably a taped lecture describing facilities and
synchronized to color slides. Purchase of a commercial
college library orientation film or film series could supplement this. Audio visual materials, not equipment and its
maintenance, should be part of the library's materials
collection.

All possible techniques should be utilized to bring the
community college student and library together. Student
library handbooks should be developed and distributed
free as part of every registration. In addition to regulations,
layouts, resources, etc., they should provide work-sheets.

Although not essential to the support of a community
college library program, a successful library technology
program can be one of the community college library's
contributions to its institution's unique provisions. Diplo-
mates of a library technology curriculum are needed in
many areas. It must, however, be judged in relation to
community needs, remuneration and legislation, and to
community college teaching staff and opportunity for learning experiences.

Faculty library orientation and handbook should be
provided. It has been shown that many teachers have
little or no skill in utilizing library resources. Their reliance
on the textbook, which does little to foster library-class
integration, general reading or critical thinking is related
in part to their backgrounds. This is especially true of
some community college teachers. Library orientation and
handbook use should provide some assistance.

It should be recognized that the community college library
should not and cannot serve as a public library. The
typical community college library is not as yet able to
serve its own clientele adequately. This arrangement inhibits
development of public library service, and neither the college
nor the public library is geared to provide adequately for
the two distinct clienteles.

Librarians should continue to strive toward improved
community college library programing through membership in professional organizations and local and national

activities. For their part, professional groups representing library service, the junior college and public education should work together towards realization of their mutual goals. A joint, ongoing committee representing the American Association of Junior Colleges and the Association of College and Research Libraries would be a good start. There are implications for schools of education and professional library service. Classes, workshops, conferences and consultation services should be further developed in the areas of community college library service, administration, instructional materials and audio visual. Continued progress in teacher education which is more library-oriented than in the past will improve the situation at all levels of public education.

Budget statistics and the great shortages of librarians and books portray inadequate community college libraries which have survived because of unique approaches and clever techniques. Adequate support of the library program is important to all departments of the community college. The needs of other departments may also be insatiable, but theirs tend to present themselves in direct relationship to specific advancements of the institution and its curricula. The library is not, and must avoid being thought of as, a competitor with other departments for funds. While each community college's goals are unique, there are many similarities and common problems faced in effective library programing. Within the present decade, community college library programs should be enabled to develop commensurately with their institution's expansion. While working towards these conservative recommendations, the vision of the ultimate goal must be kept in sight.

Characteristics of an Ideal Community College Library Program

There follows a description of the ideal community college library program — the fully functioning one which amply supports the unique institution of which it is a part. Admittedly the description is incomplete, as it is impossible to describe fully any or all of its components without reference to a particular situation, but the reader will catch a glimpse of a community college library program functioning effectively.

A capable library director has been a member of the community college faculty since a year before first classes. His selection was based on training which includes a fifth-year accredited library degree as well as considerable relevant experience. He has faculty status equivalent to departmental chairman, is responsible for presenting and administering the library budget, materials and staff selection, and is an active member of college committees. His staff includes a clerk-typist who has been employed since the start of planning. Soon after, an experienced cataloger began to supervise the processing of acquisitions and maintenance of the collection and card catalog. Another librarian began to plan the readers' advisory program about three months before first classes.

The reader's adviser is responsible for an instructional program which includes testing, orientation, an instruction course and classroom work. With the library director, he maintains a public relations program of student, faculty and community relationships by such means as displays, open house, consultation and participation in the college advisee program. Another member of the professional library staff is qualified to supervise the audio visual program and is able to devote his full time to it. He has ample technical assistance. All of the professional library staff are active in community college and library activities. Additional library staff members are provided as the enrollment increases, the community college emphases change and programs develop.

Library clerks are equal in salary and status to other college clerks, thereby providing better qualified library personnel. Clerks are employed in an approximate ratio of one to each librarian. The library director has the assistance of a full-time secretary. Student employees shelve, shelf-read and do errands. The reader's adviser or one of the other librarians, one clerk and one page are on duty at all times that the library is open. Frequent staff meetings and conferences with the library director are held.

The centrally and conveniently located community college library building was one of the first on the new campus. It includes two library classrooms adjacent to the main library and the audio visual facilities, open stacks with a capacity of 30,000 volumes and expansion, a browsing room, conference and typing roomettes, storage facilities, separate library office, staff work-rooms, a main reading room and areas for circulation activities, periodicals, reserves and reference. The library is convenient to the parking lot and it also houses the faculty lounge. Various areas of student use and the construction of the library building itself, as well as a college student lounge and study halls elsewhere, permit either silence or conversation in the library. The building was planned with professional library consultation, and the library director worked with the architects, who were experienced in college library construction. They have provided a controlled single-exit flow of traffic and seating for 25% of the anticipated full-time-equivalent enrollment. A variety of seating arrangements includes many study carrels, lounge-type accommodations in the browsing room, as well as standard work tables and chairs. The building attracts the new student as a cordial, comfortable and efficient environment. It is air-conditioned, bright and planned on the module. The concept of centralization of all materials is clear. The audio visual program is housed here and audio visual materials are part of the library collection. There are preview-listening roomettes as well as workrooms for students. Teachers are encouraged to schedule classes in the audio visual classroom, although films can be used in the class buildings. Preparation of an orientation series of colored slides synchronized with a taped lecture is an example of the integrated library-audio visual programs' work.

Community college faculty are educators experienced in integrating library use with their teaching as well as in the many ways of fostering student library attitude open to them alone. They have fulfilled local certification requirements, which include library and audio visual preparation. Each faculty member has at least one conference each semester with the reader's adviser to discuss such things as use to be made and being made of his reserves, development of the library collection and program and library-classroom instruction. He feels free to arrange further discussions with both the reader's adviser and the library director. He has come to realize that, because of a collection which is adequate quantitatively and qualitatively and required instruction in library usage, students can be encouraged

and required to utilize library resources more broadly than
in the past or elsewhere. He has therefore decreased his
use of reserves and requires students to purchase some
paperbacks, read broadly and do independent research. The
English Department cooperates in the follow-up work needed
in connection with the library's testing program. A faculty
library handbook is frequently revised and other library
publications also aim to fill the teacher's needs. Departmental
chairmen study book requests made by their staffs and
channel them to the library director. The library is able to
borrow from specialized libraries in the community in behalf
of faculty members because it has resources to loan in
return. Faculty book requests and recommendations reflect
knowledge of the library's collection and current acquisitions, as well as an interest in developing the library collection beyond personal interests.

The community college library program has had the
support of an ALA Standards-budget since the start of the
college. Initially its budget was assigned to capital expenditure until Standards were met. Now, after five years, it has
been decreased to a minimum of 5% of the college budget,
exclusive of audio visual expenditures. Departmental allocations are not necessary — faculty know that, wherever
possible, books they request specifically will be acquired.
Administration and departmental chairmen know that book
selection and coordination of the collection and acquisitions
are most wisely left in the hands of the library director.

The community college administration is interested, informed and accessible in regard to library matters. It therefore provides funds and authority with which to carry out
the program and policy developed by the library director
and studied jointly by them. It is familiar with the ALA
Standards and supports them. Earlier, the president recruited his library director a year before first classes. He
continues to place emphasis on recruiting exceptionally
well-qualified faculty. The library director is responsible
to the college president, particularly with regard to finances
and management of the library program. The dean of
instruction and he work closely regarding academic matters.
The library director is a member of the curriculum and
academic policy committees.

The library's collecting policy is based on two principles —

the community college library should provide for all of its students' needs and all materials should be centralized in one library collection. The library director does not hesitate to acquire all types of materials regardless of format, subject matter and reading levels. Audio visual materials are listed in the card catalog. The book collection contained 20,000 titles at the time of first classes, including a strong reference collection. The work was made possible by an adequate library staff on hand before first classes, use of a commercial processing service for part of the collection and purchase of a 10,000-cataloged-titles package for another part. The collection has grown and been weeded steadily as enrollment and programs expanded and changed. Books and journals listed in the indexes subscribed to are routinely acquired. (BIBLIOGRAPHIC INDEX, BIOGRAPHY INDEX, BOOK REVIEW DIGEST, CUMULATIVE BOOK INDEX, ESSAY AND GENERAL LITERATURE INDEX, INTERNATIONAL INDEX, LIBRARY LITERATURE and READERS' GUIDE TO PERIODICAL LITERATURE are basics; depending on program emphases, two or more of AGRICULTURAL INDEX, APPLIED SCIENCE AND TECHNOLOGY INDEX, ART INDEX, BUSINESS PERIODICALS INDEX AND EDUCATION INDEX.) Five years of three hundred recent periodical titles circulate from supervised shelves. Earlier issues are on microfilm. The browsing collection of new books and current periodicals attracts students. Education and other professional books housed in the general library collection's open stacks bring students, books and faculty closer in this environment. The library functions as a college archive.

The community college library is entirely independent of other libraries, but it cooperates with the county public library system as a reference education library. Library purchasing is handled in whatever manner the library director deems most productive and efficient. Library space and staff are not usurped for or by other parts of the community college.

Much emphasis is placed by community college library staff on student library use. The reader's adviser's mission lies in this area. A testing program in cooperation with the guidance department provides the opportunity of exemption for some new full-time students from the required library instruction course, as well as planning information for librarians and teachers. Other students may attend orientation sessions given at the beginning of each semester. The student library handbook is revised and publicized regularly. Classroom instruction relating current topics to library use and specialized tools is solicited by instructors. The library classrooms are in almost constant use. The possibility of a library technology course is being studied in relation to community needs and in cooperation with other local organizations.

The library program is regarded by community college students and faculty with satisfaction and respect. There is pride in such a program because there is recognition of its need and its importance in the total community college program.

NOTES

1. American Association of Junior Colleges. JUNIOR COLLEGE DIRECTORY. Washington, The Association, 1962.
2. Bogue, Jesse Parker. THE COMMUNITY COLLEGE. New York, McGraw-Hill, 1950. p.xx.
3. LOOK 24:26-8, December 6, 1960.
4. NEWSWEEK 53:69, March 23, 1959.
5. U. S. NEWS & WORLD REPORT 44:77-80, May 2, 1958.
6. Morrison, Duncan G. and S.V. Martorana. THE 2-YEAR COMMUNITY COLLEGE, AN ANNOTATED LIST OF STUDIES AND SURVEYS. BULLETIN 1958, NO. 14. Washington, U. S. Office of Education, 1958. Page 3.
7. Fields, Ralph R. THE COMMUNITY COLLEGE MOVEMENT. New York, McGraw-Hill, 1962.
   Medsker, Leland L. JUNIOR COLLEGE: PROGRESS AND PROSPECT. New York, McGraw-Hill, 1960.
   Thornton, James W. COMMUNITY JUNIOR COLLEGE. New York, Wiley, 1960.
8. Lyle, Guy Redvers. ADMINISTRATION OF THE COLLEGE LIBRARY, 3 ed. New York, Wilson, 1961. p. 21.
9. American Library Association. Association of College and Research Libraries. "ALA Standards for Junior College Libraries," COLLEGE & RESEARCH LIBRARIES 21:200-206, May 1960.
10. American Association of Junior Colleges. Commission on Administration. REPORT OF THE SUBCOMMITTEE STUDYING 'STANDARDS FOR JUNIOR COLLEGE LIBRARIES.' PUBLISHED MAY 1960, BY THE AMERICAN LIBRARY ASSOCIATION, Washington, The Commission, 1961.
11. From a letter to the writer, dated March 14, 1963, from Jesse R. Barnet, Staff Associate, American Association of Junior Colleges.

12. American Library Association. Association of College and Research Libraries. "ALA Standards for Junior College Libraries," COLLEGE & RESEARCH LIBRARIES 21:200-206, May 1960.

13. Wilson, Louis Round and Maurice Falcolm Tauber. THE UNIVERSITY LIBRARY — THE ORGANIZATION, ADMINISTRATION, AND FUNCTIONS OF ACADEMIC LIBRARIES, 2 ed. New York, Columbia University Press, 1956. p. 96-7.

14. American Library Association. Association of College and Research Libraries. "ALA Standards for Junior College Libraries," COLLEGE & RESEARCH LIBRARIES 21:200-206, May 1960. p. 200.

15. ALA BULLETIN. Cover. Volume 56, September 1962.

16. Adams, Harlen. THE JUNIOR COLLEGE LIBRARY PROGRAM, A STUDY OF LIBRARY SERVICES IN RELATION TO INSTRUCTIONAL PROCEDURES. Chicago, American Library Association, 1940. p. 1, 2.

17. American Library Association. Association of College and Research Libraries. "ALA Standards for Junior College Libraries," COLLEGE & RESEARCH LIBRARIES 21:200-206, May 1960. p. 200.

18. Knapp, Patricia B. PROJECT 874 COOPERATIVE RESEARCH BRANCH, OFFICE OF EDUCATION: AN EXPERIMENT IN COORDINATION BETWEEN TEACHING AND LIBRARY STAFF FOR CHANGING STUDENT USE OF LIBRARY RESOURCES. Washington, U. S. Office of Education, Proposal approved March 1, 1960.

19. Knapp, Patricia B. COLLEGE TEACHING AND THE COLLEGE LIBRARY; ACRL MONOGRAPH NO. 23. Chicago, American Library Association, 1959.

20. Wilson, Louis Round. THE LIBRARY IN COLLEGE INSTRUCTION. New York, Wilson, 1951.

21. Southern Association of Colleges and Secondary Schools. Committee on Work Conferences on Higher Education. HIGHER EDUCATION IN THE SOUTH. Chapel Hill, University of North Carolina Press, 1947. p. 130-43.

22. Parsons, Mary D. "The College Library: Storehouse or Laboratory?," ANTHOLOGY MCC 1956: STUDIES, ESSAYS AND POEMS BY FACULTY MEMBERS OF MEXICO CITY COLLEGE, PRESENTED AS A CONTRIBUTION TO THE SEVENTH MEXICAN BOOK FAIR. Mexico, Mexico City College Press, 1956. p. 296.

23. Feagley, Ethel Margaret et al. A LIBRARY ORIENTATION TEST FOR COLLEGE FRESHMEN. New York, Bureau of Publications, Teachers College, 1955.

24. Cook, Margaret Gerry. THE NEW LIBRARY KEY, 2 ed. New York, Wilson, 1963.
25. American Library Association. Association of College and Research Libraries. "ALA Standards for Junior College Libraries," COLLEGE Y RESEARCH LIBRARIES 21:200-206, May 1960. p. 200.
26. Lyle, Guy Redvers. ADMINISTRATION OF THE COLLEGE LIBRARY, 3 ed. New York, Wilson, 1961. p. 21.
27. Wriston, Henry M. "The College Librarian and the Teaching Staff," ALA BULLETIN 29:177-182, April 1935. p. 178.
28. Bishop, William Warner. "Library Service in the Junior College," JUNIOR COLLEGE JOURNAL 8:456-461, May 1935. p. 457.
29. Johnson, Byron Lamar. GENERAL EDUCATION IN ACTION. Washington, American Council on Education, 1952. p. 328-9.
30. Branscomb, Bennett Harvie. TEACHING WITH BOOKS; A STUDY OF COLLEGE LIBRARIES. Chicago, American Library Association, 1940. p. 84.
31. Jones, Robert C. THE ADMINISTRATIVE RELATIONSHIPS OF THE LIBRARY AND THE JUNIOR COLLEGE. Doctoral dissertation, University of Denver, 1958.
32. Lyle, Guy Redvers. ADMINISTRATION OF THE COLLEGE LIBRARY, 3 ed. New York, Wilson, 1961. p. 50.
33. Thornton, Eileen. "Libraries in Smaller Institutions of Higher Education," p. 191-208 In Schick, Frank Leopold, FUTURE OF LIBRARY SERVICE: DEMOGRAPHIC ASPECTS AND IMPLICATIONS. Urbana, Ill., Graduate School of Library Service, 1962. p. 199.
34. Southern Association of Colleges and Secondary Schools. Committee on Work Conferences on Higher Education. HIGHER EDUCATION IN THE SOUTH. Chapel Hill, University of North Carolina Press, 1947. p. 139.
35. Johnson, Byron Lamar. GENERAL EDUCATION IN ACTION. Washington, American Council on Education, 1952. p. 329.
36. Branscomb, Bennett Harvie. TEACHING WITH BOOKS; A STUDY OF COLLEGE LIBRARIES. Chicago, American Library Association, 1940. p. 98.
37. Good, Carter Victor. DICTIONARY OF EDUCATION; PREPARED UNDER THE AUSPICES OF PHI DELTA KAPPA, 2 ed. New York, McGraw, 1959. p. 197.
38. Hechinger, Fred M. "No Place to Read: Book Shortage in Schools Blamed for Libraries' Traffic Jams," NEW YORK TIMES, Sunday, April 21, 1963. p. E7.

DATA OBTAINED FROM THE QUESTIONNAIRE

	ANALYSIS	
	Number of Responses (103)	Percent of total Response (100%)
1. Community college environment		
Urban	57	55.3%
Suburban	30	29.1
Rural	12	11.6
Other	4	3.9

2.3. Other community library service

Distance to nearest public library:

close (within walking distance)	36	34.9
1-5 miles	59	57.2
6-10 miles	5	4.8
not reported, or none	3	2.9

Approximate number of volumes in
public library:

under 10,000	7
10,001-20,000	8
20,001-50,000	25
50,001-75,000	5
75,001-100,000	10
over 100,000	16

Formal arrangements established
between community college

ANALYSIS
Number   Percent
of   of total
Responses Response
(103)   (100%)

library and public library (in
order of frequency):
    exchange lists &/or materials
    inter-library loan
    present ID (or public library) card
    union catalog participation
    plan to buy to avoid excessive duplication
    public library discards to college
    share membership in bibliographic center
    none formal — all informal
    none: aim to provide all students' needs

Other libraries accessible to
  community college:
    state university &/or college   35
    county   25
    high school   7
    municipal   5
    special, or other   51

4. Sharing of the community college library

Share complete facilities   39   37.8%
Do not share   62   60.1
No reply   2   1.9
  Description of the sharing:
    share with high school   15
    collections available to
      community for reference   13
    collections available to
      community for reference &
      circulation   13
    community unrestricted but
      high school reference only   8
    share with a teachers college,
      4-year college, university etc.   5
    share with public library   1
    alumnae may use   1
  Opinion of sharing arrangement(s):
    unacceptable   18
    acceptable   31
    misc. qualified answers   3

	ANALYSIS	
	Number of Responses (103)	Percent of total Response (100%)

5. Pre-planning

Library planning begun one year
before first classes:

some	13	12.6%
none	64	62.1
unknown (institution too old etc.)	26	28.2

Library consultant employed in pre-planning:

yes	5	4.8%
no	67	65.
unknown (too old, no records etc.)	18	17.4
no reply	13	12.6

Description of the pre-planning:
librarian employed before
opening   9
library developed from a high
school or high school/com-
munity college combination   8
college purchased materials
from a former library   3

6. Evaluation of the current library program

Current library program evaluated by
professional library survey:

yes	20	19.4%
no	67	65.
no reply	16	15.5

Areas of recommendations of the
survey:
increase collection/quantity and
quality
increase staff
increase facilities, including
seating
increase collection/quality
increase collection/quantity

	ANALYSIS	
	Number of Responses (103)	Percent of total Response (100%)

increase circulation, use
separate high school and community
   college libraries
increase budget
weed collection
self-evaluate as preparation for
   accreditation

Library cooperatively planned by faculty,
  administration, students, interested laymen:

some	96	93.2%
little or none	4	3.8
temporary planning group for new bldg. etc.	3	2.9

Description of the cooperative
planning:
  faculty library committee
  students involved
  book purchases recommended by
    faculty, students, library staff
  library director member of
    administrative all-college
    planning group (preference
    expressed)
  administrator-library director
  "much talk — no action"
  planning group for new building
  alumnae drive for books

Recent innovations, modifications in library
  program:

some	75	72.8%
"continued growth process" philosophy	8	7.7
none	20	19.4

Description of principal innovations,
modifications:
  building/facilities improvement
  increase in hours
  microfilm periodicals

	ANALYSIS	
	Number of Responses (103)	Percent of total Response (100%)

orientation program
audio visual improvement
paperback holdings: sell, bind
separation of community college
   & other libraries
commercial processing of materials
new charging/circulation procedure
open stacks
library instruction course
Docustat (inexpensive, self-service
   photo reproduction)
library committee statement on censorship
curtailment of high school use
classified catalog
Library of Congress classification

Recommendations made by accreditation
   visitors:

some	62	61.1%
none	30	29.1
not relevant (not yet visited etc.)	11	10.8

Description of recommendations:
   increase facilities, including
      seating
   increase staff
   increase collection/quantity
   increase budget
   increase library use by faculty
   audio visual improvement
   departmental allocations
   increase collection/quality
   separate community college and
      high school libraries
   library committee — innovate or
      activate
   increase library director's status
      &/or salary
   increase circulation, use
   bind periodicals
   increase hours

	ANALYSIS	
	Number of Responses (103)	Percent of total Response (100%)

orientation program
utilize library standards
faculty participate in building
   collection
librarian on duty at all times
   library is open

ALA Standards utilized:

yes	81	78.6%
no	11	10.6
no comment	11	10.6

Opinion of ALA Standards:

good, helpful guideposts	44	42.7%
not high enough	10	9.7
good, but not easily applicable everywhere	10	9.7
utilized by library director but not by administration	9	8.7
too qualitative; prefer more quantitative	6	5.8
helpful with administration and public	5	4.8
wish state, regional, junior college etc. associations would adopt	5	4.8
not acquainted	4	3.8
problem to get administrative support; they consider state & regional standards	3	2.9
too high	3	2.9
use regional and state also	2	1.9
too quantitative; prefer more qualitative	1	.9
undecided	1	.9

7. Library committee

yes	71	68.9%
no	29	28.1
no reply	3	2.9

ANALYSIS

	Number of Responses (103)	Percent of total Response (100%)

Make-up of the library committee:
  represent faculty
  student participation
  no library representation
  anyone interested
  administration and library director

Function of the library committee:

advisory	32
not defined	21
review book acquisitions	6
dictate policy and practice	5
policy-making	4
accreditation &/or self-study	2
temporary: new building	1

Effectiveness of the library committee:

no comment	42
ineffectual	12
effectual "depending . . ."	11
"capable, interested, effective"	6

Library directors' added comments:
  not needed here: all-college (other)
    active committee on which library
    director serves
  opposed
  later — for future

Appointed by:

chief administrator	35
dean	19
committee	9
library director	2
departmental chairman	1
other	5

Place of library director on committee:

chairman	32
member	17
secretary	10

	ANALYSIS	
	Number of Responses (103)	Percent of total Response (100%)
exofficio	7	
honorary only	2	
none	2	
co-chairman	1	

8. Library materials for faculty use

Teachers' materials included in library
collection:

yes	82	79.6%
no	12	11.6
no reply	9	8.7

Use of these materials by faculty:

extensive	17	
occasional	52	
infrequent	13	

JUNIOR COLLEGE JOURNAL
subscription placed:

yes	93	90.2%
no	3	2.9
no reply	7	6.7

Back files of JUNIOR COLLEGE
JOURNAL on hand:

yes	92	89.3%
no	4	3.8
no reply	7	6.7

Inter-library cooperation supported:

yes	83	80.5%
no	10	9.7
no reply, or "aim to provide our needs"	10	9.7

Inter-library cooperation mainly
in behalf of:

faculty	53	
students	11	
both faculty and students	19	

| | ANALYSIS | |
	Number of Responses (103)	Percent of total Response (100%)

9. Library publications (see also question 9)

News bulletins, book-lists etc.
distributed:

yes	96	93.2%
no	5	4.8
no reply	2	1.9

10. Library instruction

Library handbook regularly
distributed:

yes	44	42.7%
no	48	46.6
no reply	11	10.6

Library orientation test administered
to all new students:

yes	15	14.5
no	77	74.7
no reply	11	10.7

Orientation attendance required of new
students:

yes	58	56.3%
no	37	35.9
other	8	7.7

Implementation of orientation:

in freshman English class	35
part of freshman orientation course	12
during freshman orientation week program	11

Evaluation of orientation:

not adequate in library director's opinion	55
provision adequate	16

Audio visual materials utilized in
library instruction:

yes	15	14.5%

	ANALYSIS	
	Number of Responses (103)	Percent of total Response (100%)
no	77	74.7
no reply	11	10.7
Description of audio visual materials utilized in library orientation and instruction:		
none	71	68.9%
comment on lack of suitable available	12	11.6
charts, strips, slides but not film	9	8.7
commercial film(s)	6	5.8
locally made for local needs	3	2.9
for the future	2	1.9
THE NEW LIBRARY KEY or other similar publication included in freshman English materials:		
yes	14	13.5%
no	77	74.
no comment	12	11.6
Library instruction fostered in connection with coursework:		
some	69	66.9%
none	19	18.4
other	15	14.5
In subject areas: English social sciences sciences technologies humanities other		
Efforts, aside from reserves, made by instructors to integrate library use and coursework:		
some	44	42.7%
little or none	53	51.4
no reply	6	5.8

	ANALYSIS	
	Number of Responses (103)	Percent of total Response (100%)

Description:
  reference problems assigned
  routine: e.g. display book jackets
  up to librarian to effect
    integration
  syllabi &/or reading lists kept at
    library desk
  librarian invited to lecture to
    class
  hold class in or bring class to
    library
  have librarian make up
    bibliographies
  library unit in course
  special course shelves
  check up on use made of reserves

Library instruction provided in a college
  course:

yes	19	18.4%
no	77	74.7
no reply	7	6.7

  Course taught by:

library director	9
other professional library staff	9
librarian and English teacher	1

  Description of course:

for library clerk preparation	6
for transfer students mainly	6
to influence career choice	3
purpose not stated	3
part of local night school	1

Library technology curriculum provides
  library instruction:

yes	4	3.8%
no	90	87.3
no reply	9	8.7

| | ANALYSIS | |
| | Number of Responses (103) | Percent of total Response (100%) |

Comments on library technology curriculum:
  future possibility — 6
  opposed — not collegiate — 1

11. "Reaching students" in other ways

Library-audio visual club sponsored by library:

yes	1	.9%
no	95	92.2
no reply	7	6.7

Participation in discussion groups etc. facilitated by library program:

yes	28	27.1%
no	63	61.1
other	12	11.6

  Description:
    displays etc.
    not possible in present set-up;
      for future
    Great Books group
    provide meeting space
    college program already too full
    radio or tv program
    book club or talks

Library work-as-a-career fostered:

yes	64	62.1%
no	23	22.3
no reply	16	15.5

  Description (See also 12, 13):
    informal, personal contact
    influence student assistants
    displays etc.
    Careers Day on campus
    formal counseling &/or
      cooperation with counseling
      department

| | ANALYSIS | |
	Number of Responses (103)	Percent of total Response (100%)
take students to library schools, conferences		
National Library Week observance		
Student-purchase of books encouraged:		
yes	31	30. %
qualified no: no time, staff, facilities	21	20.3
no	51	49.5

Description:
  college bookstore sells paperbacks
  library sells paperbacks or
    plans to
  paperback fair regular event; contest
  library recommends titles for
    stock-in bookstore
  library has discontinued selling
    paperbacks

Students required to purchase textbooks:		
yes	91	88.3%
no	2	1.9
no reply	10	9.7

12. Organization of the collection

Library holdings organized as one coordinated collection:		
yes	94	91.2%
no	4	3.8
no reply	5	4.8

Departmental, division, or other collections:		
yes	19	18.4%
no	56	54.3
no reply	28	27.1

	ANALYSIS	
	Number of Responses (103)	Percent of total Response (100%)
College resource materials centrally, fully cataloged:		
yes	71	68.9%
no	16	15.5
no reply	16	15.5
Library considered an "instructional materials center":		
yes	68	66. %
no	23	22.3
"more than **instructional** materials"	12	11.6
Library materials represent a variety of format i.e. books, films, filmstrips, slides, recordings, periodicals, pamphlets:		
yes	65	63.1%
no	21	20.3
no reply	17	16.5

    Other types not listed above:
        microfilm
        paintings, reproductions, prints
        maps, globes
        tapes
        documents
        clippings
        programs
        transparencies
        charts
        plates

13. Collection coverage

All materials needed in the students' work provided by collection:		
yes	42	40.7%
no	57	55.3
no reply	4	3.8

	ANALYSIS	
	Number of Responses (103)	Percent of total Response (100%)
Need for average student to use other libraries:		
extensive	11	10.6%
occasional	70	67.9
infrequent	19	18.4
Students' borrowing patterns:		
mainly from general collection	40	38.8%
mainly from reserves	56	54.3
varied	3	2.9
no reply	4	3.8
Coverage in depth and extent exceeding immediate requirements of the students provided by library collection:		
some	59	57.2%
little or none	7	6.7
fail to understand question	2	1.9
no comment	35	33.9

Description of provision:
wide subject coverage
adequate general collection
quantitatively and qualitatively and professional book
selection
adequate book budget and
professional book selection
build up collection quantitatively
utilize basic book lists
buy for the future
little or none
must fall back on interloan
faculty active in book selection
and know collection
departmental allocations and
limited budget prevent
making this provision
fail to understand question

ANALYSIS
Number   Percent
of   of total
Responses   Response
(103)   (100%)

borrow from high school to
    supplement
buy below and beyond junior
    college level
readers' advisory service

Provision of the library collection for
  coverage sufficient to stimulate best
  students and to serve faculty:

yes	67	65. %
no	27	26.2
no reply	9	8.7

Evidence offered that there is
  no such provision:

have less than 20,000 volumes	7
often just don't have the needed book	5
need more funds	4
statistics	4
collection is curriculum-weighted	2
faculty & students request inter-loan & permission to use other libraries too often	2
lack of use	1
collection & budget have not increased with enrollment & budget request increase	1
must limit books loaned	1

Evidence offered that there is
  such provision:

comments of faculty and students	19
statistics	13
no evidence presented	12
personal opinion	8
graduates return to use library	8

	ANALYSIS	
	Number of Responses (103)	Percent of total Response (100%)
can supply all requests	5	
other	2	
Collection contains a minimum of 20,000 volumes:		
yes	38	36.8%
no	65	63.1
If no, library has this goal:		
yes	61	
no — unable because of lack of space	4	
Number cataloged **volumes** in collection:		
1-5,000	5	4.8%
5,001-10,000	23	22.3
10,001-15,000	21	20.3
15,001-19,999	16	15.5
20,000 plus	38	36.8
Number **volumes** added in first five years of college:		
1-5,000	14	13.5%
5,001-10,000	25	24.2
10,001-15,000	5	4.8
15,001-17,000	2	1.9
less than five years old	20	19.4
not stated	37	35.9
Continuation orders placed for basic, standard references & bibliographic tools e.g.:		
READERS' GUIDE	98	
BOOK REVIEW DIGEST	93	
CUMULATIVE BOOK INDEX	88	
GRANGER'S INDEX TO POETRY	80	
ESSAY & GENERAL LITERATURE INDEX	78	

	ANALYSIS	
	Number of Responses (103)	Percent of total Response (100%)
BIOGRAPHY INDEX	70	
EDUCATIONAL MEDIA INDEX	34	
EDUCATORS GUIDE TO FREE FILMS	All opposed, or fail to reply.	

Others added by community
  colleges:

EDUCATION INDEX	20
INTERNATIONAL INDEX	18
APPLIED SCIENCE & TECHNOLOGY INDEX	10
BUSINESS PERIODICALS INDEX	7
NEW YORK TIMES INDEX	7
PAIS, ART INDEX, BIO- LOGICAL ABSTRACTS (each)	4/12
VERTICAL FILE INDEX, BIBLIOGRAPHIC INDEX (each)	3/6
CHEM ABSTRACTS, INDEX MEDICUS, TECHNI- CAL BOOK REVIEW INDEX, ENGINEER- ING INDEX, PSYCH ABSTRACTS, PLAY INDEX (each)	2/12

Provision for keeping collection up-to-
  date:

yes	74	71.8%
no	11	10.6
no reply	18	17.4

Description of the provision:
  professional book selection i.e.

	ANALYSIS Number of Responses (103)	Percent of total Response (100%)

systematic continual perusal
of review media, regular
ordering, utilization of basic
bibliographies, knowledge of
collection etc.
regular weeding and follow-up
not possible because of
inadequate funds
query departments regularly
faculty examine their sections
continuations, standing orders
buy new editions, discard old;
rotate encyclopediae every
5 years
adequate budget
dept. allocations prevent doing
this
regular inventory and follow-up
dept. allocations facilitate this
other

Policy regarding:
Purchase of duplicates

minimize	21	20.3%
as needed in opinion of library director	20	19.4
on a maximum basis e.g. up to 8	14	13.5
instructor-request	11	10.6
on a per student formula e.g. 1/20	10	9.7
for reserve collection only	10	9.7
no policy	7	6.7
favor duplication	2	1.9
other	8	7.7

Use of gifts

evaluate & accept with "no strings"	79	76.6%
accept	10	9.7
no policy	4	3.8
store	2	1.9
send to United States Book Exchange	1	.9

	ANALYSIS	
	Number of Responses (103)	Percent of total Response (100%)
at library director's discretion	1	.9
library director & president's joint decision	1	.9
other	5	4.8
Inventory:		
annual	53	51.4%
cover every 2 years	13	12.6
no policy	13	12.6
no time/staff	5	4.8
cover every 3 years	4	3.8
semestral	3	2.9
spot check &/or only reserves or reference	3	2.9
rotation — continuous	2	1.9
section every year	2	1.9
cover every four years	1	.9
other	4	3.8
Textbook acquisition (& textbook use) in the college:		
do not purchase	39	37.8%
do not purchase if in college course use	14	13.5
minimize	10	9.7
no policy	9	8.7
instructor-request	7	6.7
1 copy each	3	2.9
for reference	2	1.9
accept as gifts only	1	.9
for faculty use	1	.9
other	17	16.5
Reserve collections:		
instructor-request	82	79.6%
established by student need in library director's judgment	6	5.8
minimize	5	4.8
to preserve certain materials	2	1.9
1/10	2	1.9

	ANALYSIS	
	Number of Responses (103)	Percent of total Response (100%)
no policy	1	.9
"open reserves"	1	.9
remove if not used	1	.9
other, or no reply	3	2.9

Out-of-print book use

no policy — as needed and available	52	50.4%
instructor-request	17	16.5
must substitute — not enough staff, funds	9	8.7
minimize	4	3.8
buying arrangements with county preclude	1	.9
items listed in standard references only	1	.9
other, or no reply	19	18.4

Paperbacks:
only if not available in other
format; then must bind
only if not available in other
format
no policy
library sells paperbacks or
plans to
minimize
recreational browsing collection —
not cataloged
use as gifts
fiction only
must get 2 copies to justify
cataloging cost
instructor-request
only to replace out-of-print books

Use of standardized bibliographies ("basic bibliographies") in book selection:

routine procedure	50	48.5%
use all available, but a new one is needed in the field; all available contain out of print references	15	14.5

	ANALYSIS	
	Number of Responses (103)	Percent of total Response (100%)
no policy	8	7.7
little or no use	5	4.8
time permitting	5	4.8
use with discretion	5	4.8
misunderstood question — thought it referred to reviewing media	4	3.8
use for reference materials	1	.9
use for specialized materials	1	.9
other	9	8.7

14. Collection: Periodicals

Number of titles regularly received:		
1-50	4	3.8%
51-100	15	14.5
101-150	18	17.4
151-200	17	16.5
over 200	5	4.8
no report	44	42.7

Number of titles regularly received in foreign languages:		
1-5	56	54.3%
6-10	19	18.4
11-15	2	1.9
over 15	3	2.9
none	18	17.4
no reply	5	4.8

Number of newspaper titles regularly received:		
1-5	23	22.3%
6-10	41	39.8
11-15	19	18.4
over 15	8	7.7
none	3	2.9
no reply	9	8.7

| | ANALYSIS | |
	Number of Responses (103)	Percent of total Response (100%)

15. Audio visual materials and services

Audio visual materials and services
provided by community college
library program:

yes	39	37.8%
no	42	40.7
no reply	22	21.3

If no, dept. of college through
which they are administered:
"audio visual" (non-

library)	17	
other	25	

Comfortable facilities for previewing
films, listening to recordings etc. in
the library:

yes	35	33.9%
no	38	36.8
no reply	30	29.1

Part of a film library, pool,
district office, or other cen-

tralized group	12	

16. Library quarters

Centrally and conveniently located:

yes	77	74.7%
no	22	21.3
no reply	4	3.8

Separate building occupied by library
(although not necessarily a library
building):

yes	54	52.4%
no	49	47.5

Share library with a high school or

another library or institution:	39	37.8%

	ANALYSIS	
	Number of Responses (103)	Percent of total Response (100%)
Have separate library workroom:	74	71.8%
More than one public library room:	51	49.5
Building fireproof or resistant:	75	72.8
Building air-conditioned:	35	33.9
Number of volumes which can be added to present facilities i.e. without an addition, new building or construction:		
1-500	3	2.9%
501-1,000	5	4.8
1,001-1,500	5	4.8
1,501-2,000	11	10.6
over 2,000	68	66.
none	5	4.8
no reply	6	5.8
Separate student lounge facilities provided by college:		
yes	87	84.4
no	16	15.5

17. Provision for "practical competence" i.e. technology as well as transfer students, and others:

Provision for vocational guidance included in collection and services:		
yes	91	88.3%
no	7	6.7
no reply	5	4.8

Description of the provision:
  comprehensive college catalog
    collection
  pamphlets
  educational and vocational
    guidance materials in
    counseling center/person-
    nel office

	ANALYSIS	
	Number of Responses (103)	Percent of total Response (100%)

CAREERS RESEARCH
  MONOGRAPHS
government documents
commercial and state employment office
series
SCIENCE RESEARCH
  ASSOCIATES series
"corner," "room"
an indexed (pamphlet) file
CHRONICLE GUIDANCE
  SERVICE subscription

Fiction and biography featured:

yes	92	89.3%
no	4	3.8
no reply	7	6.7

Reading improvement, study skills
  etc. provided for in collection:

yes	45	43.6%
no	43	41.7
no reply	15	14.5

Form:
  reading machines, remedial reading
    materials
  easy-to-read books in all subjects
    but on mature level i.e. pro-
    fessional book selection
  English-as-a-second-language
    materials
  little or none
  study skills materials
  special reading lists
  readers' advisory
  phonograph records
  several editions of same title
  "how to" books and vocabulary
    builders

	ANALYSIS	
	Number of Responses (103)	Percent of total Response (100%)

young people's encyclopediae
   circulate
other

Comfortable and attractive browsing
   area in library:

yes	47	45.6%
no	46	44.6
no reply	10	9.7

Special efforts made by instructors,
   other than reserves, to encourage
   general reading:

some	39	37.8%
little or none	27	26.2
no reply	37	35.9

Description:

little or none	27
routine lip-service e.g. display book jackets	15
give extra credit	6
reading lists	4
read extensively and are genuinely professional and enthusiastic in their work	3
discuss new library acquisitions	2
encourage student purchase of books	2
remedial reading	1
supplementary readings	1
discussion groups	1
other	4

18. Technical processes

System of classification utilized:

Library of Congress	4	3.8%

	ANALYSIS	
	Number of Responses (103)	Percent of total Response (100%)
Dewey	96	93.2
no reply	3	2.9
Subject-headings utilized:		
Library of Congress	57	55.3%
Sears	31	30.
LC/Sears	11	10.6
no reply	4	3.8
Catalog cards purchased:		
yes	91	88.3%
no	6	5.8
no reply	6	5.8
System of circulation control:		
not stated	57	55.3%
Gaylord	12	11.6
turnstyle &/or door-check	5	4.8
keysort	4	3.8
Newark	4	3.8
none	1	.9
IBM	1	.9
other	19	18.4
Person in charge of card catalog, technical processes:		
library director	31	30. %
cataloger	27	26.2
assistant librarian	20	19.4
none or not stated	20	19.4
a clerk	5	4.8
Participation in centralized cataloging &/or patronize commercial book-processing service:		
yes	11	10.6%
no	85	82.5
no comment	7	6.7
Description:		
Alanar	7	

| | ANALYSIS | |
	Number of Responses (103)	Percent of total Response (100%)
centralized district cataloging program	3	
school district central office, Board of Education	1	
Open stack area utilized:		
yes	99	96.1%
no	1	.9
no comment	3	2.9
Periodicals circulate:		
yes	68	66. %
no	31	30.
no reply	4	3.8
Description:		
unbound issues only	36	
overnight only	31	
bound volumes only	1	
Ample reserve materials provided:		
yes	77	74.7%
no	3	2.9
realistically, this is an impossibility-type-answer	5	4.8
no reply	18	17.4
Reserve collections established		
by faculty request	82	79.6%
by student need in librarian's judgment	6	5.8
no reply	15	14.5
Library director's opinion of reserve system:		
satisfactory/adequate	35	
necessary-evil-type answer	20	
favors	8	
overdone by instructors	8	
unsatisfactory/inadequate	4	
opposed	4	

	ANALYSIS	
	Number of Responses (103)	Percent of total Response (100%)
encourages mutilation and stealing under pressure	3	
prefer use of subject assign- ments and no reserves	2	
depends on faculty cooperation	2	
haven't enough books to abandon it	1	
should be only one of several reading encouragement devices	1	

Library hours:

open as many hours as needed in library director's opinion	72	69.9%
not open sufficient hours	16	15.5
no reply	15	14.5

Staff provision at time hours were last extended:

some	54	52.4%
none	22	21.3
no comment or not relevant	27	26.2

Seating for 25% of full-time-equivalent enrollment provided:

yes	23	22.3%
no	77	74.7

Seating for less than 25% enrollment:

1-5%	7
6-10%	22
11-15%	13
16%-20%	15
21-24%	5
less than 25% but unknown	15

Noise, student conduct etc. in library:

not a major problem	20	19.4%

	ANALYSIS	
	Number of Responses (103)	Percent of total Response (100%)
a problem	38	36.8
no comment	45	43.6

Comment on noise, student conduct,
   etc.:
     constant problem
     no problem
     have zones of quiet,
       conversation, silence etc.
     will be better in new building
     not enough staff to make
       possible conditions conducive
       to library use
     "students want and need quiet"
     "librarians must act as
       policemen"
     "nature of community college
       student requires that there be
       supervision"
     lack of study places other than
       library cause of problem
     lack of student lounge one
       cause of problem

19. Library management

Library director reports to college president:		
yes	60	58.2%
no	39	37.8
no reply	4	3.8
Library director reports to dean	28	27.1
Library director reports to vice president	5	4.8
Library director reports to other	6	5.8
Library director responsible for preparation of library budget:		
yes	76	73.7%

| | ANALYSIS | |
	Number of Responses (103)	Percent of total Response (100%)
no	20	19.4
no reply	7	6.7
Library director responsible for recruitment of library staff:		
yes	58	56.3%
no	27	26.2
no reply	18	17.4
Library director member of college committees:		
yes	81	78.6%
no	12	11.6
no reply	10	9.7
Description of committee activities (other than library committee):		
curriculum committee	33	
"senate" or other major, all-college group	14	
audio visual committee	2	
other, including library committee	32	
Library director responsible for book selection and expenditures:		
yes	63	61.1%
qualified yes: "voluntary" departmental allocations	30	29.1
no	5	4.8
no reply	5	4.8
Departmental allocations; library director restricted:		
yes	30	29.1%
no	64	62.1
no reply	9	8.7

	ANALYSIS	
	Number of Responses (103)	Percent of total Response (100%)

20. Library staff

Total professional staff:

"1/2"	1	.9%
1	31	30.
2	34	30.
3	20	19.4
4	5	4.8
5	6	5.8
6	1	.9
7	2	1.9
8	-	-
9	1	.9
unknown, or none	2	1.9

At least 2 professional librarians on staff:

yes	69	66.9%
no	34	33.

All professional librarians hold 5th-year library degree or more (Note: includes 32 community colleges with only one librarian on staff; includes accredited and unaccredited institutions of training.)

	64	62.1%

Total clerical staff:

1	19	18.4%
2	21	20.3
3	11	10.6
4	10	9.7
5	7	6.7
6	9	8.7
7	-	-
8	2	1.9
9	1	.9
10	-	-
more than 10	1	.9
none, or unknown	22	21.3

	ANALYSIS	
	Number of Responses (103)	Percent of total Response (100%)
Ratio of professional/clerical:		
50/50	50	48.5%
not able to establish from data	20	19.4
professional predominates excessively	18	17.4
clerical predominates excessively	15	14.5
Entire library staff consists of		
respondent	32	31.
Presence of staff member other than library director with specific audio visual responsibility (although not necessarily training &/or experience)	23	22.3
Professional training of library director:		
5th-year library degree or more/ accredited	69	66.9%
5th-year library degree/not accredited	10	9.7
other library training	11	10.6
no library training	3	2.9
vacancy	3	2.9
no information	7	6.7
Professional library staff have faculty status:		
yes — all	85	82.5%
none	7	6.7
unknown	10	9.7
library director/yes; other librarians/no	1	.9
library director chairman of division or department	13	12.6%
At least 2 staff members, 1 of whom is a librarian, on duty at all times library is open:		
yes	35	33.9%
no	61	59.2
no reply	7	6.7

	ANALYSIS	
	Number of Responses (103)	Percent of total Response (100%)
Number of student assistants employed (part-time; hours vary):		
1-5	43	41.7%
over 5	45	43.6
no reply	15	14.5
Student-workers regularly alone on duty in the library:		
yes	37	35.9%
no	60	58.2
no reply	6	5.8
Student-workers regularly alone on duty at the circulation desk:		
yes	61	59.2%
no	28	27.1
no reply	14	13.5

Library director's opinion of above student-staff pattern:	
need more full time staff	28
satisfactory	21
best we can do resigned-type answer	11
bad	11
retraining is a constant problem and waste	8
there should always be a librarian on duty	6
students should never be alone on duty at the circulation desk	4

21. Finances

Library budget % of college budget:		
1-4%	51	49.5%
5% or more	36	34.9
not available	16	15.5

| | ANALYSIS | |
	Number of Responses (103)	Percent of total Response (100%)
Per student expenditure of the total college budget for library program:		
$1-10	8	7.7%
11-20	41	39.2
21-30	19	18.4
31-40	4	3.8
41-50	6	5.8
over $50	2	1.9
not available	23	22.3
Library budget:		
$1-10,000	6	5.8%
10,001-20,000	28	27.1
20,001-30,000	19	18.4
30,001-40,000	15	14.5
40,001-50,000	10	9.7
50,001-60,000	5	4.8
60,001-70,000	4	3.8
70,001-80,000	3	2.9
80,001-90,000	3	2.9
90,001-100,000	2	1.9
100,001-110,000	3	2.9
110,001-120,000	-	-
120,001-130,000	2	1.9
unknown	3	2.9

22. Illustrative ways in which community college library programs support the unique functions of their institutions, as reported by library directors.

By circulating reference-type material to help students who work and leave school early.

By knowing our students better, partly from living in the same area, partly because school is still small.

By having special technical books for community-sponsored apprentice programs.

By having materials on the economic activities of the area and the historical records of the area.

By having a flexible materials collection.

By serving as a college cultural center.

By serving as a community cultural center.

By assisting in the development of discrimination and understanding.

By assisting in the growth and refinement of education and training instead of the usual 'reading for recreation etc.'

By functioning as a materials center, teaching agency and reading center.

By offering service comparable to the senior college our students are likely to attend upon graduation from this community college; terminal students also need the experience of having superior library service available to them **now** — their habits of library use throughout their lives depend upon the experience they have now.

By providing any resident with library reference use (California law).

By providing a quiet place for study.

By stimulating growth of the individual who cannot find materials in his public library.

By serving the community as a scholarly library.

By working to increase the overlap of what were two separate lists of ways in which our library program supports the college functions — the ways in which I feel it should and the ways our teachers and dean think it should!

By requiring library orientation now (hope to go into a course next year).

23. Problem areas in community college library service as reported by library directors, with illustrative statements by them.

Staff

It is hard to sell administrators the idea of adding staff members to give more or better service — they haven't added more teachers, so why can't the library take care of the enrollment?

The greatest problem in community college library service is adequacy of resources, and by this I mean a **staff** and services are the library's resources as much as its book collection. Since two-year colleges are a rather recent phenomenon on the American education scene, they are all experiencing these growing pains. The recent Standards will help a lot toward solving this problem.

We also need auxiliary help, not necessarily professional, but with a cultural background. Intelligent and trained student assistants are fine **except** that the turnover is too great in a junior college and individual training cost on the job is too high. We have thought of having an accredited class, required for would-be assistants, on library use and resources using work projects in the library as part of the course, and then putting students on the payroll second semester. Perhaps we could get a reservoir of help that way. Often our student assistants seem to continue their interest in library work as a profession when they go to senior college.

Staff too small to supervise library for the hours the library is required to be open.

The greatest problem areas are: . . . convincing the administration of the college of the necessity of having well-trained personnel:
   (a) placing teachers in the library who do not have training has created library problems . . . ;
   (b) library clerks are not given compensation equivalent to personnel in other departments e.g. the accounting office and the registrar's office;
   (c) to date, I have been unable to convince the administration of the necessity of having at least three different classifications for clerks . . .

A solution would be state and national funds made available for junior college libraries.

Students should not be in a position over their peers.

Retraining student workers is a constant problem and waste.

There should always be a librarian on duty.

Physical facilities: housing, seating, storage etc.

The community college should have its own campus and own library, and not just be 'more high school.' Unless it has its own campus — apart — and maintains regular college standards, with outside lecturers invited etc. and a faculty that is geared to college teaching, it will just be a continuation of high school.

We need to run fast enough to stand still.

Faculty-library relations

The faculty does not make periodic and thorough checks on their areas.

Some faculty, promoted to a junior college after years of high school teaching, sometimes bring their high school teaching ways with them. Their assignments do not have the breadth and scope that require much library research and delving into books. The student does not become adept in library research.

Stimulating faculty use (and thereby student use also) of the library and its facilities (is a problem).

Many faculty members tend to stay with the landmark books of their subject-matters for years; they are still recommending and using titles which were outstanding when they were undergraduates (even in science).

Many instructors lack the special training and experience needed in the community college.

(A problem) is the instructor who gives required readings and informs the library after the class. It's the same story everywhere, I know, **but** there are more part-time faculty in the community college.

Budget finances etc.

If the money is available and the librarian has had experience, there seems to be no excuse for a poor community college library program.

(There is) insufficient budgetary support to provide reasonable standards of library service.

Financial help from the state and federal governments is needed.

Money is the big problem, but as far as the community college movement is concerned the background to this need lies in the unwillingness of school officials to recognize the ways in which a college (junior college too) needs a good library. I think the worst thing that ever happened to most junior colleges is that they are run generally by local school boards.

Interpreting procedures to administration so that they can understand budget needs (is a problem). This applies also to the setting up of a junior college library. Numbers loom large. Staff is often deemed superfluous if its hours exceed the 'open hours' of the library. A new junior college should not be allowed to open without sufficient library holdings, and this means hiring a cataloging-acquisitions librarian and some clerical staff at least a year in advance to assure the 10,000-20,000 volume stock being ready to circulate on opening day. They think this is a large number and forget the reference-type books which do not circulate and can only be used for spot research.

Methods of purchasing materials for the library should be re-evaluated and restrictions removed.

Additional funds for building library book stock in first ten years (are needed).

Our problem is to get a big enough budget to get the necessary basic collection we should have right now. We buy used books via want-lists and bindable paperbacks to help.

Administration-library relations

Recognition of library staff as professional personnel (is needed).

The inability of many administrators to realize that a college program cannot be met with a library that is too small in volumes and understaffed (is a problem). A high school library is not a college library, and a book collection of under 20-30,000 volumes is not adequate, nor can any junior or community college provide adequate service with only one librarian and no clerical staff. All the problems in junior college libraries go back to administrative failures.

The criticisms made by the AJC Commission on Administration reveal an alarming lack of knowledge of college library functions and confusion with high school on the part of the presidents and administrators.

Convincing the administration of the purpose and place of the library in the total program and providing the money necessary to provide this program (is a problem).

Lack of a clear notion on the part of the administration and governing board concerning the relation of the library to the functions of the college, and reluctance on the part of the administration to calculate the budgetary requirements of the functions that are assigned to the library are related again to a lack of clear policy on the quality of education which the college is attempting to provide.

Pressure on governing boards and administrators from outside the college is needed to raise library standards.

(A problem is) lack of administrative understanding of library needs and possibilities in a non-library minded region isolated from metropolitan services, with poor to non-existing elementary and high school library services.

Librarians try to get the Standards over to administration and get nowhere until much later, (accreditation) recommendations are along more or less the same lines.

The problem is to get administrative support; . . . they consider state and regional standards . . . wish state, regional, junior college associations would adopt them (i.e. ALA Standards.)

When faced with the fact that money is the crucial ingredient lacking, it is simpler for them to attribute the situation to **our** not having developed a new librarianship!

There is a great lack of communication.

After **months** of trying to take the initiative in communication, and **years** of trying to convey the picture, his reply now is 'Yes, but there just aren't funds now.'

Most administrators have come from the classroom and understand the problems of the instructional departments.

Administrators seek solutions to problems and to correct specific situations — unfortunately, the library — if it is successful — is never completely 'solved.' Library problems merely change and are never settled. The librarian's problem is to face up to the need to lead the college president.

Collection and its organization

(There is) too little available literature and nonapplicable to our situation when located.

The greatest problem seems to be the community's wishing to use the college library as an adjunct to the public library. We have had many planning meetings with the public librarians of the area to determine how we can best afford our proper services to our patrons without duplicating each others' collections, thereby sharing our tax dollars.

Providing adequate reference service for our students and teaching them to use the library efficiently (are problems.)

Materials seem no particular problem if enough budget is available.

Centralization of audio visual materials under a trained audio visual specialist (is needed.)

Just what should a junior college library contain — how much top-level high school material, how much scholarly upper-class and reserve materials? Should it be cataloged simply or with a university library's precision in classifying? How much good textbook material should it accept for reserve use, and should all old editions be discarded?

(Reserves) should be only one of several reading encouragement devices; encourages stealing under pressure and mutilation — overdone by instructors — depends on faculty cooperation.

The reserve system is a necessary evil — **evil** because it encourages dishonesty when great pressure is exerted upon a class to read the same material — **necessary** because of inadequate collection and faculty dependence upon it.

Minimum standards are useful only when they are interpreted as general guidelines for the resources needed to meet the minimum needs of an average institution — specialized curricula demand far more library materials.

Balancing materials for terminal programs, especially technologies, liberal arts transfer program, and the individual needs is a challenge, not a problem.

It is impossible for us to depend on other libraries for our needs. English teachers used to send classes to nearby private research libraries — now they are excluded because there were too many and they did not know how to use the facilities.

Definition of functions

The principal problem in a community college library is the problem which derives from the ambivalent nature of the community college itself. It must serve terminal as well as transfer students. As I see it, the library for such a college must go farther than the junior college library to make available to its terminal students materials to which they would have been exposed in a regular four-year college. Transfer students should also be offered some opportunity to gain at least sight familiarity with tools they will be expected to know as juniors in a four year college.

The abilities and reading interests of high school and junior college students are too far apart to be compatible (in the joint library situation).

Institutions utilizing modern methods of teaching, study, and reading call for increased library services and large book collections.

Our student body is not prepared to use **any** library.

The audio visual equipment was simply assigned to the library with no staff provision. We lack a technician. Faculty resent having to operate the machines and blame the library of course. There is waste in repair cost.

Student library use and instruction

The next problem is getting proper use of library materials from a freshman-sophomore clientele who have enough trouble getting through the textbook much less reading something from the library. This too must be solved if we are to prepare these people for the tremendous outside reading load that will be put upon them in upper class years at the universities.

Because young people are anxious to get away from home and into the popular universities, the community college so often does not get the cross section of the better students — only those who need to take advantage of the financial saving. I feel that more worthwhile social and intellectually stimulating activities on the college level might help in this area. The library suffers most of all because the public is unaware or uninformed about its contribution to the community through the lives of the students. Open house, exhibits, lectures, book reviews might help if they were permitted or if there were money available.

How can students be stimulated to a consistent program of extra-curricular reading?

Our evening opening is largely nullified for hundreds of students in such a large territory.

The greatest problem area to me is student attendance in the library: our students do not stay on campus after class and consequently do not make the use that could be made of the library resources which exist.

Too high a proportion of student body of low aptitude and immature or poorly motivated to permit maintenance of a noise level of a senior college.

A library technology as you call it is not collegiate.

Students want and need quiet.

Librarians must act as policemen.

The nature of the community college student requires that there be supervision.

Our student body is not prepared to use any library.

The community college is just more high school, so the college library is more high school library.

Other

There is a great need for books or other publications on organizing and administering junior/community college libraries.

The Standards serve as a guide to the junior college librarian in evaluating a given library in terms of staff, resources, services — they probably receive scant attention from administrators and are of little value in pressuring for additional staff, funds etc.

The 'psychologist' displays and distributes so-called vocational guidance materials although he apparently cannot distinguish between commercial mailings and factual presentation, between advertisements and relevant information. The students are confused by what they read as well as by the impression they receive thusly that all vocational material is free for the taking!

I am still swamped with the problems inherited from a library which was supposedly established when I was hired; the faculty had spent what funds there were on books at random, a clerk 'cataloged' them — three years later and I cope with the faculty and student resentments — this is called salvage.

24. Aspects of an "ideal" community college library program of the future, as reported by library directors, with illustrative statements by them.

Staff

(We should have) regional workshops in reference and other library techniques for upgrading and refreshing library personnel, one college unit per week of appropriate work, and instruction by outstanding practitioners in teams on Saturdays.

There is a great need for professional readers' advisory service available at all times the library is open — in the community college this could provide: consultation with faculty regarding orientation, bibliographies, reserves, interloans, professional collections, research etc.; students' reference assistance; special lectures, class visits, faculty and student orientation, and instruction; sponsorship of clubs and discussion groups; displays and bulletin boards; vocational, personal and educational guidance . . .

A capable librarian and an ALA Standard-budget are all that are needed.

. . . We have thought of having an accredited class, required for would-be (student) assistants, on library use and resources using work projects in the library as part of the course, and then putting students on the payroll second semester. Perhaps we could get a reservoir of help that way.

Physical facilities: housing, seating, storage etc.

Our aims (include a) classroomsize area opening into library which can be used for library instruction, film previewing, or faculty study.

We also use microfilm extensively to preserve back files of magazines. Most two-year college libraries are not saddled with extensive back files of old bound magazines, so they can really start saving magazines on film and thus avoid future storage problems that are sure to develop otherwise.

Combination of student lounge — study hall separate from the library — adequate seating in library — professional librarian on duty — areas where conversation and silence can both be expected — study carrels and browsing area (is our goal some day).

A library classroom, workroom, study carrels, conference and typing rooms, browsing room, controlled exit in a library building . . .

Budget, finances etc.

Elimination of departmental allocations (is needed).

Capable library director and ALA Standards-budget are all that are needed.

Faculty-library relations

(We should aim) to make the library an integral part of the instructional program. This will probably require some reorganization of instructional methods — less reliance on lectures, more on individual study, less rigidity in class and assignment scheduling. The focus should be on learning rather than on teaching, and teachers should become librarians and librarians teachers, in B. Lamar Johnson's phrase. Book selection and use of the library would become phases of the same problem.

A voluntary library committee of enthusiastic teachers with the librarian as chairman (is needed).

Every faculty member have a conference with a librarian each semester to discuss use made and to be made in his area of reserves for instance (would be ideal).

Full time faculty will more likely have their first loyalty to the community college.

Collection and its organization

Possibly (we should aim) to make the library the scholarly division of a county-wide public library system, but with caution and proper organization in order to prevent harm to registered students.

(We should have) five years' unbound periodicals circulating from supervised open shelves; microcards of older periodicals needing to be circulated, with inexpensive hand readers; periodicals of lasting reference value on microfilm; micro-color where needed; and microreader with dime-slot printer.

Definition of functions

Our ideal is to make the library in reality 'the heart of the college', a strong audio visual program after careful planning has been done concerning direction and growth of this program, adequate seating space for students and faculty, improved system of circulation control, an organized collection of college archives, an improved catalog with complete revision of filing and recataloging where necessary, and improved service to students and faculty.

Student library use and instruction

First, I would like to incorporate a library instruction course for all freshmen, with some credit attached to it, to inform students how to use the information at their fingertips.

Introduction of vocational library clerk program on an academic basis as another terminal vocational course (is a goal).

The nature of the community college student and the impossibility of providing adequate library orientation are such that a course should be required of all new students.

Combination of student lounge — study hall separate from the library — adequate seating in the library — professional librarian on duty — areas where conversation and silence can both be expected — study carrels and browsing area (is our ideal).

Other

Have the library take over the leadership in the development and presentation of cultural events on campus e.g. lectures, book talks, private-library contests etc.

25. Areas of community college library program need today, as ranked by library directors.

Note: Almost without exception, participants in this question drew attention to the fact that problem (or success) areas derive from **budgetary** provision.

The eleven categories ranked below were presented at random and the respondent was asked to rank them as to "areas of community college library program need today":

Rank	Area(s)
1	Budget. Staff.
2	Seating.
3	Collection/quality.
4	Collection/quantity. Faculty relationships. Administration relationships.
5	Evaluation of program.
6	Definition of functions.
7	Housing.
8	Storage facilities.

Questionnaire on Public Community College Library Practices

Helen Wheeler
January 1, 1963

It is suggested that you read through the questionnaire completely before answering.
Two copies are enclosed. Please return one completed copy at your earliest convenience
to the following address:

Miss Helen R. Wheeler
500 Riverside Drive
New York 27, New York

A stamped, addressed envelope is enclosed. You may keep the second copy for your files.

* *

Community college_____
Address_____
Name & title of person completing questionnaire_____
Date_____

If you do not consider that your institution functions as a public community college,
please state that fact and return this questionnaire.

1. Is your community college urban?_____Suburban?_____Rural?_____Other?_____

2. Is a library fee charged?_____If so, how much?_____

3. How far is the nearest public library?_____Is it open evenings?_____Weekends?_____
    Approx. number of volumes in public library._____What formal arrangements have
    been established between the public (and/or other) and community college libraries?

    Other libraries readily accessible to community college students and faculty?_____

4. Are the community college library facilities, collection, personnel, or services shared
    with any other institution or clientele?_____Please describe._____

    What is your opinion of this arrangement?_____

-2-

5. Is the current library program the result of planning which began at least one year
    before first classes were enrolled?_____Describe._____

    Was a library consultant employed in pre-planning?_____Please name him/her._____

6. Has the current library program been evaluated by means of the professional library
    survey?_____In what areas were recommendations made?_____

    Are the results being implemented?_____Please describe._____

    What forms of cooperative library planning by community college faculty, administra-
    tion, students, and interested laymen exist?_____

    What innovations or experimental procedures are currently being tested by the library?

    What and when was the last major modification of the library program?_____

    In the last accrediting visit, were there specific recommendations for the college
    library?_____What were they?_____

    Are they being carried out?_____Please describe their implementation._____

    Are the guidelines for evaluation provided by the American Library Association's
    "Standards for Junior College Libraries"[1] being utilized?_____What is your opinion
    of the new Standards?_____

_____

1. ALA Standards for Jr. College Libraries... INC&RL xxi:200-6, May '60.

FACSIMILE OF THE QUESTIONNAIRE   147

-3-

7. Is there a library committee?_____If so, what are its make-up, functions, and effective-
    ness?_____

        Appointed by whom?_____Place of the library director on the com-
        mittee?_____

8. Does the library include teachers' materials in subject areas?_____In education?_____
    In audio visual?_____In community college?_____Are there separate professional col-
    lections?_____For each, please describe use and importance._____

        Do faculty regularly make recommendations in these areas?_____Are these materials
        utilized extensively?_____occasionally?_____infrequently?_____Does the library
        subscribe to The Junior College Journal?_____Does it have back files of JCJ?_____
        Is the library involved in inter-library cooperation?_____Mainly in behalf of
        faculty?_____or of students?_____Please describe inter-library activities._____

9. Does the library distribute news bulletins and book-lists?_____Please identify and
    describe (e.g. monthly?_____weekly?_____) _____

10. Is a free library handbook given every student early in every term?_____Is A Library
    Orientation Test for College Freshmen[1](or some other instrument of this type) ad-
    ministered to all new full-time students as part of the testing program and/or
    orientation week?_____Are the results utilized in planning library instruction and
    other aspects of the college program?_____How?_____

        Is library orientation attendance required of all new full-time students early in
        the term?_____How is it implemented?_____

        What does the orientation include?_____
        In your opinion, is this adequate?_____

        Is a library orientation film part of the library collection?_____What is its title?
        (source, etc.)_____

_____

1. Feagley, Ethel. A library orientation test for college freshmen. N.Y., TC, '55.

-4-

Is a publication such as <u>The New Library Key</u>[1] part of freshman English materials?____
To what specific use is it put in English class?_____

Is library instruction fostered in connection with specific coursework throughout the
term?_____In what subject areas particularly?_____

What efforts to integrate library use and coursework are made by instructors?_____

Is a library instruction COURSE offered?_____If so, who teaches it?_____
_____How often does it meet?_____For what credit?____Elective or
required?_____Please describe._____

Is there a curriculum of library technology as part of the total college offerings?
_____Please comment._____

11. Does the library sponsor a library-audio visual club?_____Please describe its activi-
     ties._____

Does the library facilitate participation in discussion groups concerned with significant books, films, and ideas?_____Please describe._____

Does it foster librarianship as a career?_____By what means?_____

Does it encourage student purchase of books, especially paperback editions, through
such activity as publicity for <u>Paperback Books In Print</u>?_____Please comment._____

Do students generally purchase at least one textbook for each course?_____Or does the
college provide them (free)?_____Please comment._____

---

1. Cook, Margaret. The new library key. N.Y., Wilson, '56.

12. Are the library holdings one coordinated collection?_____Are there departmental, di-
    visional, or other collections?_____Are all college resource materials centrally and
    fully cataloged?_____

    Is the college library considered an instructional materials center?_____Do library
    materials represent a variety of format i.e. books, films, filmstrips, slides,
    recordings, periodicals, pamphlets?_____(Add others.)_____

13. In your judgment, does the library collection provide ALL materials needed in the
    ordinary course of the students' work?_____Is it necessary for the average student
    to use other libraries extensively?_____occasionally?_____infrequently?_____

    Are the majority of inter-library loans made by or for the college library?_____
    Does the average student borrow "Reserve" books more frequently than books from the
    general collection?_____Please describe the students' borrowing pattern(s)._____

    What provision is made to provide coverage in depth and extent exceeding the im-
    mediate requirements of the students?_____

    In your judgment, does the library collection provide coverage sufficient to stimulate
    the best students and to serve the faculty?_____What evidence do you have of this?

    Does it contain a minimum of 20,000 volumes?_____If not, does the library clearly
    have this as a working-goal?_____Number of volumes in the library (include only
    cataloged items; if combined with high school, public, or other library, state number
    procured especially for the community college library)_____Number of
    volumes added during the community college library's first five years_____
    the past five years._____
    Has the library placed continuation orders for basic, standard reference and biblio-
    graphic-control tools, such as those listed below (add others):

    Biography Index_____   Book Review Digest_____
    Cumulative Book Index_____   Essay & General Literature Index_____
    Granger's Index to Poetry_____   Readers' Guide_____
    Educational Media Index_____   Educators Guide to Free Films_____

Is there special provision for keeping the collection up-to-date?_____Please describe.

What policy has been adopted with respect to:
   Purchase of duplicates_____

   Use of gifts_____

   Inventory_____

   Textbook acquisition (and textbook use in the college)_____

   Reserve collections_____

   Out of print books_____

   Paperbacks_____

   Use of standardized bibliographies in book selection_____

14. Number of periodicals (total) regularly received._____
    Approximate number in other languages received regularly._____
           "   "   regularly bound._____
           "   "   of newspapers currently received._____
    Does the library regularly receive all titles indexed in Readers' Guide?_____

15. Does the library provide the college audio visual materials?_____services?_____
    materials and services?_____If not, through what college department are they ad-
    ministered?_____Are there comfortable facilities for previewing films, listening
    to recordings, etc?_____In the library?_____Please describe._____

16. Is the library centrally and conveniently located?_____In a separate library building?
    _____In room(s) in a building used for other purposes?_____Separately from a high
    school, community, or other library unit?_____Is there a separate, staff workroom?
    _____Is there more than one public library room?_____How many?_____Is building fire-
    resistant (or fireproof)?_____Air conditioned?_____
    How many books can be added without an addition to building or space now allotted to
    library?_____Does the college have a separate student lounge?_____

17. How many new instructional films are purchased each year for the technology programs?
    _____In your judgment, how well do the library collection and services provide
    for practical competence in other ways as well?_____

    What evidence do you have of this?_____

Do the library collection and services include vocational guidance materials?_____
Please describe._____

Do they include a comprehensive college and schools catalog collection?_____Do the
library collection and services feature fiction and biography in addition to the
traditional non-fiction areas?_____How are they cataloged?_____

How are they shelved?_____

Do the library collection and services provide help for the slower student in im-
proving reading and study skills?_____What form does this take?_____

Is there a comfortable and attractive browsing area?_____What special efforts to
encourage general reading, apart from required readings and setting up of "Reserves",
are being made by instructors?_____

18. System of classification used._____
    System of subject-heading._____
    Are catalog cards purchased?_____
    System of circulation-control._____

    Is there an up-to-date card catalog, with entries for materials on order, ample sub-
    ject guides and analytics?_____Title of staff member in charge of maintenance of the
    card catalog._____Does the library participate in centralized
    cataloging or patronize a commercial book-processing service?_____Please describe.

    Is there an open stack area?_____Is there a large collection of reference books on
    open shelves?_____Do periodicals circulate?_____Under what conditions?_____

    Is there an ample supply of reserve materials to meet special needs?_____How are
    reserve collections established?_____

    Your opinion of reserve system._____

    Library schedule:
    In your judgment, is the library open to its public for as many hours as are needed?
    _____(Or for more hours than are needed?_____) How and when were the current library
    hours established?_____

-8-

At the time that they were last extended, what staff provision was made?_____

Is there seating for at least 25% of the full-time equivalent student body?_____
For how many?_____Is quiet enforced on whatever level necessary for efficient and comfortable library use?_____Please comment._____

19. Do you as library director report to the college president?_____If not, to whom?
    _____Are you responsible for preparation of the library budget?
    _____For recruitment of library staff?_____Are you a member of various college com-
    mittees (e.g. curriculum)?_____Please describe these activities._____

    Do you have ultimate responsibility for book selection and expenditure of the book
    funds?_____Do you solicit and encourage recommendations from the library staff?_____
    From the college faculty?_____Are there departmental library budget allocations?_____
    If so, to what portion of the materials funds are you restricted?_____

20. Library staff
    Please list for all salaried library staff members the information requested below.

Position title	Full or part time	Training (institution and degrees)	Library experience	Teaching or other experience	Area of library responsibility and/or specialization

Do professional library staff have faculty status?_____

FACSIMILE OF THE QUESTIONNAIRE

Number of hours of paid student help per week.____Number of student assistants employed.____Are there at least two staff members, one of whom is a professional librarian, on duty at all times that the library is open to its public?____Are student workers ever alone on duty in the library?____At the circulation desk?____ What is your opinion of this staff arrangement?_____

21. What % of the college budget is the library budget?____% Total expenditure, 1961-62, for community college:

Salaries for instruction, not including library salaries $_____
Current funds for departmental use (equipment, laboratories, maps, etc.)   _____
Library purposes, including books, salaries, supplies, etc.   _____
What % of the total per student instruction cost is devoted to the acquisition of audio visual materials?____% (Does this figure include A.V. supplies and equipment?)
____

22. What do you see as the unique needs and functions of the community college movement? Which characteristics apply to your own college program and its community? In what specific ways does your library program assist in this undertaking?

23. What, in your opinion, are the greatest problem areas in community college library service in general and in your institution? Please feel free to elaborate on problems, obstacles, causes and solutions in setting up and/or maintaining a community college library program (on both the local and national levels).

24. What would you like to incorporate into your library program of the future -- ideally -- or to improve? Please describe techniques, solutions to problems, and innovations which you have found successful or observed in other community college libraries.

25. Please rank the following areas of community college library program according to need today, in your opinion:
    staff_____   seating_____   housing_____   storage
    collection (quantity)_____   collection (quality)_____   facilities_____
    definition of functions_____   evaluation of program_____
    faculty-library relationships_____   administration-library relationships_____
    budget_____   other:_____

26. Please list references to publications and articles which you have found helpful and of interest in the literature of the community college and library service, materials relating to your library and college programs, etc.

BIBLIOGRAPHY

Adams, Harlen. THE JUNIOR COLLEGE LIBRARY PROGRAM, A STUDY OF LIBRARY SERVICES IN RELATION TO INSTRUCTIONAL PROCEDURES. Chicago, American Library Association, 1940.

ALA BULLETIN. Cover, volume 56, September 1962.

American Association of Junior Colleges. JUNIOR COLLEGE DIRECTORY. Washington, The Association, 1962.

American Association of Junior Colleges. Commission on Administration. REPORT OF THE SUBCOMMITTEE STUDYING 'STANDARDS FOR JUNIOR COLLEGE LIBRARIES.' PUBLISHED MAY 1960, BY THE AMERICAN LIBRARY ASSOCIATION. Washington, The Commission, 1961.

American Council on Education. AMERICAN JUNIOR COLLEGES, 5th ed. Washington, The Council, 1960.

American Library Association. Association of College & Research Libraries. "ALA Standards for Junior College Libraries," COLLEGE & RESEARCH LIBRARIES 21:200-206, May 1960. (Also AMERICAN LIBRARY & BOOK TRADE ANNUAL, 1961. New York, Bowker, 1960. pp. 125-32.)

—— Junior College Section. "This Matter of Standards for Junior College Libraries," BULLETIN OF THE CALIFORNIA SCHOOL LIBRARY ASSOCIATION 29:9-14, May 1957.

—— Standards and Criteria Committee. GUIDELINES FOR ESTABLISHING A JUNIOR COLLEGE LIBRARY (DRAFT II, JANUARY 1963). Dearborn, Henry Ford Community College, 1963. (Norman E. Tanis, Chairman)

—— Library Administration Division. Library Organization and Management Section. Statistics Committee for College and University Libraries, comp. "College and University Library Statistics 1958/9: Junior Colleges," COLLEGE & RESEARCH LIBRARIES 21:78-88, January 1960.

Baker, Marvin Louis. A STUDY OF JUNIOR COLLEGE BUILD-
INGS AND EQUIPMENT IN THE UNITED STATES,
1955. Austin, University of Texas, 1956.

Benson, Charles Joseph. STUDY OF THE STUDENT USE OF
PERIODICALS IN A JUNIOR COLLEGE LIBRARY.
MA thesis, University of Chicago, 1955.

Bertalan, Frank J. BOOKS FOR JUNIOR COLLEGES; A LIST
OF 4,000 BOOKS, PERIODICALS, FILMS AND FILM-
STRIPS. Chicago, American Library Association, 1954.

Biermann, June "Biological Approach to the College Library,"
BULLETIN OF THE CALIFORNIA SCHOOL LI-
BRARY ASSOCIATION 32:24-6, November 1960.

Bishop, William Warner. "Library Service in the Junior College,"
JUNIOR COLLEGE JOURNAL 8:456-461, May 1935.

Bogue, Jesse Parker. THE COMMUNITY COLLEGE. New York,
McGraw-Hill, 1950.

Bowers, Sarah C. "Close Cooperation for Culture," PIONEER
(Library Bureau of Remington Rand) 21:6-7, September
1958.

Boynton, Edwin Curry. A CRITICAL ANALYSIS OF ADMINIS-
TRATIVE STAFFING NEEDS OF JUNIOR COLLEGES.
Austin, University of Texas, 1959.

Branscomb, Bennett Harvie. TEACHING WITH BOOKS; A
STUDY OF COLLEGE LIBRARIES. Chicago, American
Library Association, 1940.

Brown, Virginia C. "Spelman Memorial Library; J. Sterling Morton
Junior College, Cicero," ILLINOIS LIBRARIES 37:41-2,
February 1955.

Brubeck, Katherine McCallie. THE INFLUENCES OF THE
STANDARDS FOR JUNIOR COLLEGE LIBRARIES
OF THE JUNIOR COLLEGE LIBRARIES SECTION
OF THE ASSOCIATION OF COLLEGE AND REFER-
ENCE LIBRARIES OF THE AMERICAN LIBRARY
ASSOCIATION. Master's thesis. Tallahassee, Florida State
University, 1954.

— "Junior College Libraries," FLORIDA LIBRARIES 7:15, June
1956.

— "Junior College Libraries in Florida," FLORIDA LIBRARIES
6:14, December 1955.

California State Library, Sacramento. "California Junior College
Libraries, Annual Statistics, 1960-   ," CALIFORNIA
LIBRARY NEWS NOTES 57:104, Winter 1962-   .

Campbell, Arline Butler. WESTERN NORTH CAROLINA JU-
NIOR COLLEGE LIBRARIES: THEIR TECHNICAL
PROCEDURES AND THE POSSIBILITIES FOR CO-

OPERATION. MS in LS thesis. Chapel Hill, University of North Carolina, 1961.

"Canaveral Calling," WILSON LIBRARY BULLETIN 36:612, April 1962.

Carty, Jackson Calloway. "Survey of Administrative Standing of Head Librarians in 2-year Colleges of California," JUNIOR COLLEGE JOURNAL 29:490-2, April 1959.

Clark, Virginia. "Student Use of a Junior College Library," ILLINOIS LIBRARIES 42:316-18, May 1960.

Cook, Margaret Gerry. THE NEW LIBRARY KEY, 2 Ed. New York, Wilson, 1963.

Corcoran, Margaret M. "Springfield Junior College Library," ILLINOIS LIBRARIES 36:155-7, April 1954.

Councill, Mildred Southerland. "Problems in Organizing a Junior College Library," NORTH CAROLINA LIBRARIES 16: 47-9, February 1958.

—"Suggestions for Establishing a Small Junior College Library," JUNIOR COLLEGE JOURNAL 29:146-9, November 1958.

Crittenden, Sara Nadine. "Reference Service in the Junior College Library," NORTH CAROLINA LIBRARIES 17:80-3, Spring 1959. (Also FLORIDA LIBRARIES 8:25, March 1958).

De Los Santos, Alfredo G., Jr. "Chief Librarians of the Public Junior Colleges in Texas, 1957," TEXAS LIBRARY JOURNAL 35:25-7, March 1959.

Durham, Mary Joines. STUDY OF JUNIOR COLLEGE LIBRARIES IN GEORGIA. MA Thesis. Tallahassee, Florida State University, 1959.

Dwyer, William G. "End of an Experiment?" LIBRARY JOURNAL 87:3619-22, October 15, 1962.

Eskow, Seymour. BARRON'S GUIDE TO 2-YEAR COLLEGES. Great Neck, New York, Barron's Educational Series, Inc., 1960.

Fails, Emol Atwood. THE POTENTIAL ROLE OF PUBLIC COMMUNITY JUNIOR COLLEGES. Master's thesis. Nashville, George Peabody College for Teachers, 1956.

Feagley, Ethel Margaret et al. A LIBRARY ORIENTATION TEST FOR COLLEGE FRESHMEN. New York, Bureau of Publications, Teachers College, 1955.

Fields, Ralph R. THE COMMUNITY COLLEGE MOVEMENT. New York, McGraw-Hill, 1962.

158COMMUNITY COLLEGE LIBRARY

"Flint Junior College and Flint College, University of Michigan," Michigan," MICHIGAN LIBRARIAN 25:22-24, June 1959.

Florida State University. BASIC MATERIALS FOR FLORIDA JUNIOR COLLEGE LIBRARIES. Tallahassee, State Department of Education, Publications and Textbook Services, 1960. (Louis Shores, Editor.)

Fontane, Patrick Earl. CRITERIA FOR THE ESTABLISHMENT OF PUBLICLY-SUPPORTED COMMUNITY COLLEGES IN CONNECTICUT. Ann Arbor, University Microfilms, 1954. (Also, 1959 and 1962 supplements.)

Fordham, Leon F. "Florida's New Junior College Libraries," FLORIDA LIBRARIES 10:5-6, December 1959.

Fortenberry, W.D. "Magazine and Newspaper Reading of Junior College Freshmen," JOURNAL OF DEVELOPMENTAL READING 5: no. 1, 67-70, Autumn 1961.

Gates, Jean Key. A GUIDE TO THE USE OF BOOKS AND LIBRARIES. New York, McGraw-Hill, 1962.

Genung, Harriett. "Heart of the College," JUNIOR COLLEGE JOURNAL 24:136-46, November 1953.

Gibson, Earle Kathrun Britton FACULTY USE OF THE LIBRARY IN TEN PUBLICLY SUPPORTED JUNIOR COLLEGES IN TEXAS. MLS Thesis. Denton, Texas State College for Women, 1954.

Good, Carter Victor. DICTIONARY OF EDUCATION; PREPARED UNDER THE AUSPICES OF PHI DELTA KAPPA, 2 ed. New York, McGraw, 1959.

Greene, Robert John. LIST OF SCIENCE AND APPLIED SCIENCE BOOKS FOR FLORIDA JUNIOR COLLEGES. MS Thesis. Tallahassee, Florida State University, 1959.

Griffing, A. H. "Good Community Relations Help the Small College Library Grow," JUNIOR COLLEGE JOURNAL 30: 325-6, February 1960.

Griffith, Alice G. "Junior College Library Handbook Collection," COLLEGE & RESEARCH LIBRARIES 24:521, November 1963.

——"Library and the General Education Program in the Community College," JUNIOR COLLEGE JOURNAL 29: 486-9, April 1959.

——STANDARDS FOR THE IDEAL JUNIOR COLLEGE LIBRARY HANDBOOK. PREPARED BY THE COMMITTEE ON INSTRUCTION AND USE, JUNIOR COLLEGE LIBRARIES' SECTION, ACRL, JULY 1963.

GUIDELINES FOR ESTABLISHING JUNIOR COLLEGE LIBRARIES (PREPARED BY THE STANDARDS AND CRITERIA COMMITTEE OF ACRL'S JUNIOR COL-

LEGE LIBRARIES SECTION . . . NORMAN E. TANIS,
CHAIRMAN . . .). In College & Research Libraries 24:
501-505, November 1963.

Hardin, Maurine Sims, and H. M. Iredell. "Standards; a Challenge," BULLETIN OF THE CALIFORNIA SCHOOL
LIBRARY ASSOCIATION 24:7-24, January 1953.

Harris, Marion Dodge. "Reference Department of Los Angeles
City College Library," JUNIOR COLLEGE JOURNAL
29:222-3, December 1958.

Harvey, John F. "Role of the Junior College Library in Classroom Instruction," JUNIOR COLLEGE JOURNAL 32:
441-7, April 1962.

Hechinger, Fred M. "No Place to Read: Book Shortage in Schools
Blamed for Libraries' Traffic Jams," NEW YORK TIMES,
Sunday, April 21, 1963. p. E7.

Hillway, Tyrus. AMERICAN TWO YEAR COLLEGE. New York,
Harper, 1958.

"Hinds Junior College Library is Among Most Modern in Nation,"
MISSISSIPPI LIBRARY NEWS 26:29, March 1962.

Hirsch, Felix E. "Goals for the 1960's: the Significance of the
New ALA Standards for Junior College Libraries," JUNIOR
COLLEGE JOURNAL 31:135-9, November 1960.

— "How High Should We Aim?" ALA BULLETIN 55:160-62,
February 1961.   .

— "New Horizons for Junior College Libraries," LIBRARY
JOURNAL 85:2372-75, June 15, 1960.

Johnson, Byron Lamar. GENERAL EDUCATION IN ACTION.
Washington, American Council on Education, 1952.

— "New Junior College Library Standards — An Analysis and
Critique (with comment by Felix E. Hirsch)," ALA
BULLETIN 55:155-60, February 1961.

Johnson, Walter T. "Glance at Junior College Libraries," JUNIOR
COLLEGE JOURNAL 29:195-201, December 1958.

Jones, Robert C. THE ADMINISTRATIVE RELATIONSHIPS
OF THE LIBRARY AND THE JUNIOR COLLEGE.
Doctoral dissertation, University of Denver, 1958. (Also
"Administrative Relationships of the Library and the Junior
College," JUNIOR COLLEGE JOURNAL 29:324-8, Feb-
ruary 1959).

— "1,000 1961 BOOKS FOR THE UNDERGRADUATE COL-
LEGE LIBRARY," COLLEGE & RESEARCH LIBRA-
RIES 23:115-42, March 1962. (Also, for 1960:22:101-24,
March 1961 etc.)

—— "Use of the Library for Better Instruction," JUNIOR COLLEGE JOURNAL 29:493-5, April 1959.

Jones, William E. "Developing the Library in the Small Junior College," JUNIOR COLLEGE JOURNAL 30:149-57, November 1959.

Jordan, Robert T. "Best Books for the Lower Division College Library," LIBRARY JOURNAL 85:2535-8, July 1960.

—— "Goals — Not Standards," ALA BULLETIN 55:565-7, June 1961.

—— 750 DESIRABLE 1958 BOOKS FOR THE LOWER-DIVISION COLLEGE LIBRARY. Taft, California, Taft College Library, 1959.

JUNIOR COLLEGE DIRECTORY. Washington, American Association of Junior Colleges, annual.

"Junior College Libraries," FLORIDA LIBRARIES 11:4-5, December 1960.

"Junior College Libraries: Recommended Standards," BULLETIN OF THE CALIFORNIA SCHOOL LIBRARY ASSOCIATION 26:21-22, March 1955.

Kast, Gloria E. "Unique Junior College Library," LIBRARY JOURNAL 83:3371-2, December 1, 1958.

KEYS TO THE LIBRARY. Kugler-Barker Productions, 1951. (Kenneth Holst, 1399 North Lake Avenue, Pasadena 6, California.) 14-minute sound, black and white film. Also available in color. Rent or purchase.

Knapp, Patricia B. COLLEGE TEACHING AND THE COLLEGE LIBRARY; ACRL MONOGRAPH NO. 23. Chicago, American Library Association, 1959.

—— PROJECT 874 COOPERATIVE RESEARCH BRANCH, OFFICE OF EDUCATION: AN EXPERIMENT IN COORDINATION BETWEEN TEACHING AND LIBRARY STAFF FOR CHANGING STUDENT USE OF LIBRARY RESOURCES. Washington, U.S. Office of Education, Proposal approved March 1, 1960.

Krenitsky, Michael V. STUDY OF JUNIOR COLLEGE LIBRARIES IN TEXAS. MA Thesis, Dallas, Southern Methodist University, 1954. (Also JUNIOR COLLEGE JOURNAL 25: 331-46, February 1955.)

Krider, Marie Elder. "North Idaho Junior College Library," IDAHO LIBRARIAN 5: No. 2, April 1953, page 20.

Lash, Henry. "Paperback Revolution and the Junior College," JUNIOR COLLEGE JOURNAL 31:402-3, March 1961.

—— "Paperbacks for the Junior College; a Classified List of 1,000 Titles Costing Fifty Cents or Less," LOS ANGELES JUNIOR COLLEGE CHRONICLES, PUBLICATION NO.

680, Los Angeles City School Districts, Division of College and Adult Education, June, 1963.

Legge, Christopher Augustus Sackville. "Policies and Programs of a Small College Library," JUNIOR COLLEGE JOURNAL 29:412-13, March 1959.

LOOK 24:26-8, December 6, 1960.

Lyle, Guy Redvers. ADMINISTRATION OF THE COLLEGE LIBRARY, 3 ed. New York, Wilson, 1961.

McBirney, Ruth. "Boise Junior College Plans for New Library Building," IDAHO LIBRARIAN 15:7-8, January 1963.

McClain, Ione. "Hospital Space Becomes a Library," LIBRARY JOURNAL 82:3060-1, December 1, 1957.

Magner, Gene. "Special Collections in Junior Colleges," JUNIOR COLLEGE JOURNAL 31:345-9, February 1961.

Mapp, Edward. "Instructor-Librarian Collaboration in a Community College," JUNIOR COLLEGE JOURNAL 28: 404-6, March 1958.

— "Library in a Community College," COLLEGE & RESEARCH LIBRARIES 19:194-6, May 1958.

Martin, Elizabeth. "Foothill College Library," CALIFORNIA LIBRARIAN 24:153-8, July 1963.

Medsker, Leland L. JUNIOR COLLEGE: PROGRESS AND PROSPECT. New York, McGraw-Hill, 1960.

Melinat, Carl Herman. "Paperback Foundations: Books for Newly Established Community Colleges," LIBRARY JOURNAL 87:4466, December 15, 1962.

Miller, Sister Carlos Maria, RSM. AN EVALUATIVE SURVEY OF THE LITERATURE OF THE JUNIOR COLLEGE LIBRARY, 1925-1950. Master's thesis, Washington, Catholic University of America, 1956.

Morrison, Duncan G. "Research and the Two-year College," JUNIOR COLLEGE JOURNAL 29:128-32, November 1958.

— and S.V. Martorana. THE 2-YEAR COMMUNITY COLLEGE, AN ANNOTATED LIST OF STUDIES AND SURVEYS. BULLETIN 1958, NO. 14. Washington, U. S. Office of Education, 1958.

Murray, Thomas B. AN EVALUATION OF THE REFERENCE COLLECTIONS IN THE LIBRARIES OF SEVEN SAN FRANCISCO BAY AREA JUNIOR COLLEGES. MLS Thesis. Berkeley, University of California, 1953.

"New Simmons Library Has Opening," MISSISSIPPI LIBRARY NEWS 25:35-6, March 1961.

Newman, Ruth E. and Ira J. Peskind. "Reading Programs and the Junior College Library," COLLEGE & RESEARCH LIBRARIES 4:393-5, October 1953.

NEWSWEEK 53:69, March 23, 1959.

Obolet, Eli M. et al. COLLEGE AND UNIVERSITY LIBRARY STANDARDS — 1957 (ACRL MONOGRAPH NO. 20). Chicago, American Library Association, 1958.

Oetting, Franklin Henry. THE ROLE OF THE PUEBLO JUNIOR COLLEGE IN MEETING THE INSTITUTIONAL AND COMMUNITY NEEDS FOR AUDIO VISUAL SERVICES. Bloomington, Indiana University, 1953.

Parham, Paul. A STUDY OF SELECTED JUNIOR COLLEGE LIBRARY BUILDINGS . . . Thesis, Austin, University of Texas, 1953.

Parker, Franklin. "Community Junior College, Enfant Terrible of American Higher Education; a Bibliography of 225 Doctoral Research Dissertations," JUNIOR COLLEGE JOURNAL 32:193-204, December 1961.

Parsons, Mary D. "The College Library: Storehouse or Laboratory?" ANTHOLOGY MCC 1956: STUDIES, ESSAYS AND POEMS BY FACULTY MEMBERS OF MEXICO CITY COLLEGE, PRESENTED AS A CONTRIBUTION TO THE SEVENTH MEXICAN BOOK FAIR. Mexico, Mexico City College Press, 1956.

Pattillo, Manning M. "Appraisal of Junior College and College Libraries," COLLEGE & RESEARCH LIBRARIES 17: 397-402, September 1956.

Poteat, Dorothy Mae. BASIC LIST OF MAGAZINES FOR FLORIDA JUNIOR COLLEGES. MS Thesis. Tallahassee, Florida State University, 1959. (Also BASIC MATERIALS FOR FLORIDA JUNIOR COLLEGE LIBRARIES: MAGAZINES. See Florida State University.)

Pratt, Lula K. "Integration of the Junior College Library with Instruction," COLLEGE & RESEARCH LIBRARIES 19: 201-2, May 1958.

Praulines, Rita. COMPARISON OF VOCATIONAL GUIDANCE MATERIALS IN JUNIOR COLLEGE LIBRARIES OF CALIFORNIA AND MINNESOTA. Master's thesis. Minneapolis, University of Minnesota, 1958.

"Preparation of the Standards for Junior College Libraries," COLLEGE & RESEARCH LIBRARIES 21:199-206, May 1960.

Radner, Sanford. "Community College Reading Program," JUNIOR COLLEGE JOURNAL 30:379-80, March 1960.

Rawley, George R. THE PUBLIC SERVICES OF SELECTED
    TEXAS COLLEGE LIBRARIES. Master's thesis. Austin,
    University of Texas, 1956.

Reiman, Eva. "History of the Library at Westchester Community
    College," WESTCHESTER LIBRARY ASSOCIATION
    BULLETIN 19:17, April 1960.

REPORT OF THE DEPUTY COMMISSIONER OF EDUCA-
    CATION'S EVALUATION COMMITTEE ON THE EX-
    PERIMENTAL LIBRARY TECHNICIAN PROGRAM.
    Albany, State Education Department, New York State
    Library, 1962.

Rink, Bernard C. "Community College Library — Cultural Solar
    Plexus," COLLEGE & RESEARCH LIBRARIES 23:389-
    392, September 1962.

Rowland, Arthur Ray. "Cataloging and Classification in Junior
    College Libraries," LIBRARY RESOURCES & TECH-
    NICAL SERVICES 7:254-8, Summer 1963.

Rowland, Lois Jeannette Parker. ACTIVITIES TO ENCOUR-
    AGE EFFECTIVE USE OF LIBRARY MATERIALS
    IN JUNIOR COLLEGES. MLS thesis. Austin, University
    of Texas, 1956.

Shepard, Elizabeth. "Junior College Library Trends," NORTH
    CAROLINA LIBRARIES 14:134-6, June 1956.

Skrabak, Clement. FACULTY-LIBRARY RELATIONSHIPS IN
    TEN CALIFORNIA PUBLIC JUNIOR COLLEGES. EdD
    Thesis, Berkeley, University of California, 1953.

Smith, Floyd, Jr. "Library in the Junior College Journal: an Evalu-
    ation," JUNIOR COLLEGE JOURNAL 27:39-41, Sep-
    tember 1956.

Smith, Loy Herman and George E. McCauley. "Exhibits and Dis-
    plays in the Junior College Library," JUNIOR COLLEGE
    JOURNAL 25:354-6, February 1955.

Southern Association of Colleges and Secondary Schools. Com-
    mittee on Work Conferences on Higher Education. HIGHER
    EDUCATION IN THE SOUTH. Chapel Hill, University
    of North Carolina Press, 1947.

Tallahassee, Florida. Florida State University Library School.
    THE JUNIOR COLLEGE LIBRARY. PROCEEDINGS
    OF THE FIRST SOUTHERN COLLEGE AND RE-
    SEARCH LIBRARY WORKSHOP, PART II. FRIDAY
    MORNING, JUNE 27, 1958. Tallahassee, Florida State
    University, Library School, 1958. (Sarah Reed, Chairman.)

Tanis, Norman Earl. "Act Now: Implementing the New Junior
    College Library Standards," WILSON LIBRARY BUL-
    LETIN 35:60-1, September 1960.

— "Cooperative Program to Improve the Community College Library," JUNIOR COLLEGE JOURNAL 29:405-11, March 1959.

— "Departmental Allocation of Library Book Funds in the Junior College: Developing Criteria," LIBRARY RESOURCES & TECHNICAL SERVICES 5:321-7, Fall 1961.

— "Henry Ford Community College Library Survey," JUNIOR COLLEGE JOURNAL 30:99-105, October 1959.

— "Implementing the Junior College Library Standards," COLLEGE & RESEARCH LIBRARIES 22:130-3, March 1961.

— "Library as Part of Industrial Education," INDUSTRIAL ARTS & VOCATIONAL EDUCATION 50:17-19, April 1961.

— STRENGTHENING THE JUNIOR COLLEGE LIBRARY THROUGH USE OF THE ALA STANDARDS. Dearborn, Henry Ford Community College Library, 1962.

Thornton, Eileen. "Libraries in Smaller Institutions of Higher Education," p. 191-208 In Schick, Frank Leopold, FUTURE OF LIBRARY SERVICE: DEMOGRAPHIC ASPECTS AND IMPLICATIONS. Urbana, Ill., Graduate School of Library Service, 1962.

Thornton, James W. COMMUNITY JUNIOR COLLEGE. New York, Wiley, 1960.

— "Library in the Junior College," FLORIDA LIBRARIES 9:8-9, June 1958.

Trinkner, Charles L. BASIC BOOKS FOR JUNIOR COLLEGE LIBRARIES: 20,000 VITAL TITLES. (Volume I, Junior College Library Series). Northport, Ala., Colonial press, 1963.

— BETTER LIBRARIES MAKE BETTER SCHOOLS: CONTRIBUTIONS TO LIBRARY LITERATURE, #4. Hamden, Conn., Shoe String press, 1962.

— LIBRARY-CENTERED JUNIOR COLLEGES: BUILDINGS AND PLANS. (Volume III, Junior College Library Series.) Northport, Ala., Colonial Press, 1964.

— LIBRARY SERVICES FOR JUNIOR COLLEGES. (Volume II, Junior College Library Series). Northport, Ala., Colonial Press, 1964.

— "Library Trends in Florida's Junior Colleges," JUNIOR COLLEGE JOURNAL 30:376-8, March 1960.

U. S. NEWS & WORLD REPORT 44:77-80, May 2, 1958.

U. S. Office of Education. LIBRARY STATISTICS OF COLLEGES AND UNIVERSITIES, 1959-60; PART 2, ANALYTIC REPORT. Washington, U. S. Office of Education, Library Services Branch, 1962.

— LIBRARY STATISTICS OF COLLEGES AND UNI-
VERSITIES, 1960-61: INSTITUTIONAL DATA. Washington, U. S. Office of Education, Library Services Branch,
1962.

— LIBRARY STATISTICS OF COLLEGES AND UNI-
VERSITIES, 1961-62; PART 1, INSTITUTIONAL DATA.
Washington, U. S. Office of Education, Library Services
Branch, 1963.

Vagt, John P. COMMUNITY SERVICES OF TEXAS JUNIOR
COLLEGE LIBRARIES. MLS Thesis. Austin, University
of Texas, 1953. (Also in TEXAS LIBRARIES 17:179-82,
November 1955.)

Wallace, James O. "Junior College Libraries," JUNIOR COLLEGE
JOURNAL 25:486-7, April 1955.

Wattenbarger, James L. "Place of the Junior Community College
in the Community," FLORIDA LIBRARIES 13:5-10, September 1962.

Wetzler, John. A SURVEY OF CALIFORNIA JUNIOR COLLEGE
AUDIO VISUAL PROGRAMS. Bakersfield, Bakersfield
College, 1957.

— A SURVEY OF CALIFORNIA JUNIOR COLLEGE LI-
BRARIES. Bakersfield, Bakersfield College, 1957. (Also
BULLETIN OF THE CALIFORNIA SCHOOL LIBRARY
ASSOCIATION 29:3-6, January 1958.

Wheeler, Helen Rippier. THE COMMUNITY COLLEGE LIBRARY;
AN APPRAISAL OF CURRENT PRACTICE. New York,
Teachers College, 1964. EdD project. University Microfilm
65-4755.

— "Library Instruction and the Junior College," JUNIOR COL-
LEGE JOURNAL 31:451-2, April 1961.

White, Ruth W. "The Role of the Community College Library,"
JUNIOR COLLEGE JOURNAL 33:109-11, October 1962.

Wilson, Louis Round. THE LIBRARY IN COLLEGE INSTRUC-
TION. New York, Wilson, 1951.

— and Maurice Falcolm Tauber. THE UNIVERSITY LIBRARY
— THE ORGANIZATION, ADMINISTRATION, AND
FUNCTIONS OF ACADEMIC LIBRARIES, 2 ed. New
York, Columbia University Press, 1956.

Wriston, Henry M. "The College Librarian and the Teaching Staff,"
ALA BULLETIN 29:177-182, April 1935.

Young, Elma. "Junior College College Library Problems," BUL-
LETIN OF THE CALIFORNIA SCHOOL LIBRARY
ASSOCIATION 29:21-5, March 1958.

— BETTER LIBRARIES MAKE BETTER SCHOOLS: CON-
TRIBUTIONS TO LIBRARY LITERATURE, #4. Hamden, Conn., Shoe String press, 1962.

— LIBRARY-CENTERED JUNIOR COLLEGES: BUILD-
INGS AND PLANS. (Volume III, Junior College Library
Series.) Northport, Ala., Colonial Press, 1964.

— LIBRARY SERVICES FOR JUNIOR COLLEGES. (Volume II, Junior College Library Series). Northport, Ala.,
Colonial Press, 1964.

— "Library Trends in Florida's Junior Colleges," JUNIOR
COLLEGE JOURNAL 30:376-8, March 1960.

INDEX

Technical institute   60
Technical programs   19, 68
Testing   61
    SEE ALSO **A Library Orientation Test for College Freshmen**
Transfer   3, 17
Tuition   3, 66, 68

Vocational guidance
    SEE Guidance
"Vocational library clerk"   37

W orkroom   34, 31, 59, 64